AF486806

the internet's never-ending tragedy

LM Publishing

PO BOX 480606, Martin City, MO 64148

First Edition: December 2025

ISBN: 979-8993801605

*The word lolcow is a portmanteau of "lol" - laugh out loud
and "cow" - someone who is milked.*

*A lolcow is someone baited or tricked into responding to
trolls thereby "milking" them for amusing reactions.*

Lolcows:
The Internet's Never-Ending Tragedy

By: Luther Morgan

Preface

Right off the bat, I do not condone any harassment or other illegal activity targeted towards any person mentioned in this book. In fact, I would encourage people *not* to interact with them at all. I should also state that any additional publicity drawn to the lolcows or people mentioned is a matter of course. The people presented here have accepted being public figures. Public figures are available for public scrutiny. Still, I tried to limit the amount of time spent on personal or embarrassing topics related to people who surround the lolcows.

There will also be adult language used in this book. I have only used it as part of a direct quote.

Lolcows, as an internet phenomenon, have fascinated me for years. And when trying to describe the topic to someone who was unfamiliar with the phenomenon, I wasn't able to find a source of information to direct people to. I also wasn't able to find something that put into words the who, what, where and why - regarding lolcows. I hope that readers who are not familiar with the topic can be well acquainted through this book and readers who are very familiar with the lolcows I will discuss can learn something new.

When writing this, I wanted to be as fair and impartial as possible. In my research, I found most sources were biased. This is because most people online engage with lolcows for the purposes of getting content, amusement, and/or attention. (To be clear, there is nothing wrong with doing that.) I wanted to take a more balanced and academic approach. I wanted to study them - as objectively as possible so we can learn something from their experiences.

As part of that impartiality. I reached out to the people mentioned in the book, with available contact information, for a comment or interview. I also reached out to the lolcows we will cover. If they had something to say, I would include it.

There are a few things we will not be covering in this book. There are some people and some topics I feel are not suitable for public conversation because it could lead to more attention. The "most trolled person on the internet", Chris Chan, aka Sonichu, will not be discussed because I believe he has severe mental illness. This fact excludes him from our discussion, except for a passing mention.

Table of Contents

Introduction

Lolcows are a unique internet phenomenon. Many were once beloved online content creators who had millions of fans all over the world. To their audience, they were people to be admired, entertained by, and invested in. To YouTube, many were trailblazers or innovators of new genres of content. They became what millions aspire to be: professional YouTubers or online content creators. They were free of the rat race of a 9-to-5 job. They had their control over their own channel. They were their own boss. They could make and do whatever they wanted. The world was their oyster. Until it wasn't.

The life of the lolcow is a story of tumultuous events. A story of lies, deceit, manipulation, emotional breakdowns, crash outs, and financial ruin. The dramatic rise and fall story is familiar to us all. But unlike the fictional heroes of screen or Shakespeare, these are real life people that exist in the real world. Their real-life story is broadcast for everyone to see on the internet. And not only is it broadcast online, but there is audience participation. Anyone can comment, post, super chat, etc. and reach out to the lolcow. The internet is both a transmitter and a receiver.

The story of the lolcow is a human tragedy. In the beginning, it's a story of triumph. They reached the top of their field and rose above millions of other YouTubers. Then it becomes a story of tragedy. Their own personal flaws sowed the seeds of their destruction. The internet that brought them fame and fortune, also trapped them in a cycle of misery they can't escape.

In the book, we will explore the conditions which created the environment for the lolcow. We'll go over how lolcows are created and the traits lolcows share. We will go over the story of six selected lolcows and explore their dramatic rise and fall. I will explain why we care about them so much, their connection to archetypical tragic heroes dating back to ancient times, the hate and disgust they inspire, and their themes of eternal struggle.

Chapter 1: YouTube and Content Creators

The Beginnings of the Content Creator

The internet allowed for new kinds and forms of entertainment content not previously available in the analogue age. Early video sharing was hampered by impossibly slow download speeds for viewers and website hosting costs for creators. The old standbys of antennae, cable television, and the movie theater still reigned supreme when it came to video entertainment. Just as newspapers became irrelevant as the internet took over print, websites took over from magazines, and forums and chatrooms took over from pubs and clubs, the technological advances kept moving closer and closer to a world of online video entertainment. As internet bandwidth and computing power exponentially increased as the 20th century turned into the 21st century, it became technologically possible for video sharing websites to exist.

There was a world of three channels in the 1960s, American Broadcasting Company (ABC), Columbia Broadcasting System (CBS), and National Broadcasting Company (NBC). Then a four channel world in the 1980s as Fox Broadcasting Company (FOX) was added. By the 1990s, cable/satellite allowed additional channels. The average person now had access to 60+ channels including on-demand movies. With the power of the internet, there were now millions of possible channels. Anyone could start a "channel". In the pre-internet era, what took years of time, millions of dollars in investment, contracts with stations, and an Federal Communications Commission license, now could be done in a matter of minutes for free with the power of the internet. Every creator could have their own channel. Liberated from the traditional broadcast system, it could be tailored for each individual creator's audience.

As the internet changed from the dial up era to the broadband era, the technological limitations of the viewer on his own home computer were removed. While video sharing platforms existed before YouTube, YouTube became the de facto standard of the industry since its founding in 2005. "Broadcast Yourself" was the original motto of the site.

In its infancy, and some of these pre-2010 videos are still on the site, early internet videos were often very short, unscripted, had poor video quality, and sporadically uploaded. Many were glorified home movies. People uploaded them outside of financial motives, mainly things or topics they found interesting, amusing, informational, or educational. While it was technologically possible to share and create content between creators and viewers, it took a few years for it to become financially possible to make money off YouTube videos.

Just as technology changes and evolves, the evolution of content creation on YouTube increasingly becomes more professional. At the same time, more people were traveling to the site which allowed monetization through advertising to become increasingly viable. Within a few short years of YouTube's existence, it became financially feasible to create content on YouTube as a full-time occupation.

A "YouTuber" or "content creator" became a new sort of job which did not exist previously. A YouTuber is part author, actor, writer, producer, cinematographer, editor, and publisher. The singular person, with a singular artistic vision is at the helm and unfettered by regulation, save for the Terms of Service. While collaboration is possible for YouTubers, and many YouTubers collaborate as a form of networking and cross pollination of viewers across different channels, YouTubing can be a singular and isolated endeavor. Even the largest YouTube channels are very small operations when compared to their TV and movie counterparts. While at the same time, they can command millions of views.

Everyone knows what a YouTuber is, so I won't spend too much time explaining what it is or how it works. YouTubers make videos and people watch them. The main goals of YouTubers are to gain viewers, engagement, and subscribers. YouTubers get views from people watching their videos. People watch their videos using the algorithm to search for a video, get recommended the video in a column of suggested content, or by the subscribers page. Engagement comes from comments and liking or disliking videos. Subscribers are the dedicated audience who can view all the new videos of the creators they are subscribed to in the subscriptions tab.

YouTubers make money in various ways that are combinations reminiscent of other media. The main source of income for most channels is ad revenue through the YouTube Partner Program. Getting monetized is an early milestone for a YouTuber. They can also include sponsorships in the video itself - basically an ad built into the video. This ad read by a creator can be worth thousands, or tens of thousands of dollars for popular creators, per video.

Creators also appeal to fans directly. The most dedicated viewers will support more. This can be donations using third party websites like Patreon. It can also be in the form of merchandise, channel memberships, and super chats.

The YouTuber as a Public Figure

What was once a small corner of the internet became the dominant form of entertainment for a new generation of Americans. Starting with the Gen Xers and Millennials, YouTube and other online content platforms replaced TV as the go to at-home entertainment. While Boomers might come home from work and put on a sitcom, stay up watching late night comedy, or watch local TV news; the millennial might put on YouTube. As YouTube became a dominant force in entertainment, the creators on YouTube started becoming commercialized.

As content was professionalized, monetized, and grew in widespread acceptance, the YouTuber became a public figure. The internet is accessible to everyone and publishing yourself, or "Broadcasting Yourself" to use a YouTube parlance, by extension, made you a public figure. According to the US government, following *New York Times Co v. Sullivan, 1964*, a public figure is someone who is widely known to have influence in society. This fits with the other term for content creator: "influencer".

Like all public figures, content creators have an audience. The interactions between the audience and the YouTuber are unlike any other media. Audience interaction has been around since the earliest times. It probably always existed between the performer and the audience. In pre-industrial times, cheering, applause, booing, heckling, and throwing rotten fruit are all universally understood as audience interaction. Even across different cultures there is some way of an audience expressing its pleasure or displeasure with the performer before it.

When the newspaper and printing press were the dominant forms of media, it was very common for people to send replies to articles with a written letter. And those letters in response to the original publication were often printed in said newspaper. It was a kind of slow-motion forum posting or comments section.

This letter writing tradition continued into the movie and television era with "fan mail" and other letter writing campaigns. Such campaigns did sometimes impact studio decisions. One such example was how a letter writing campaign saved *Star Trek* in 1968. So much mail showed up in support of the show; NBC renewed it for a third season.

The audience has several ways of interacting with an online content creator. Interaction is encouraged by creators. Viewers can leave comments, and creators sometimes respond. Comments also act as a forum for people to express their opinions, similar to newspapers printing letters. Viewers could also like or dislike expressing their thumbs up or thumbs down opinion. This feature acts as a public poll for the content. Another way of interacting was response videos where other creators could make a video in response to the original video, which could go back and forth several times.

How the YouTuber appeared before the audience was also different from all other media. The YouTuber/content creator didn't come into our home from a set, film studio, sound stage, or some other expensive fabrication. Most entered our home just as they broadcast themselves from their home. Most YouTubers, particularly in the early days, had primitive studios made of a spare bedroom or basement that was then broadcast into our bedroom.

This connection and relationship between the YouTuber and the audience is different than other forms of media. It is immediate, constant, and easily accessible. A YouTuber may also not recognize they are a public figure, because from their perspective they are broadcasting from their bedroom. Even if they have hundreds of thousands or millions of views, they can go to the supermarket, run errands, etc. and never be recognized by anyone. But like all public figures, YouTubers must be careful in how they act. Because as the old adage goes, "The internet is forever".

It is well understood that public figures are treated differently in society than regular people or nonpublic figures. This perception by society is a double-edged sword. A public figure can get special treatment, but also unique ridicule and negative attention if they were to do something wrong. If John Smith walks into a restaurant, they might get treated differently than a Hollywood celebrity. Most likely they will be treated worse off. However, if a Hollywood celebrity got a DUI, it would be all over social and mainstream media. They would be derided and face criticism from millions of people. Whereas if John Smith got a DUI, it would not even make local news.

Because public figures have this constant attention on themselves, they develop mechanisms to maintain their good standing with the public and to protect their reputation. They restrict information about themselves to preserve this public image. This proves to be difficult for the YouTuber because they are supposed to be authentic and "Broadcast Yourself". This makes it a very precarious balancing act between sharing, authenticity, and audience interaction and being reserved, restricting information, and maintaining a private life.

Chapter 2: What is a Lolcow?

A troll is a person that interacts with others online in a provocative, offensive, and disruptive manner. The purpose of this provocation is usually their own amusement to mock and insult others. This can take the form of derailment, spam, and baiting outrage.

Trolling predates the internet. Other people might call it "practical jokes". Prank calls were the Boomer's/Gen Xer's version of trolling. Everyone knows the old, "is your refrigerator running? It is? You better catch it." gag. Before that there were absurd or hoax letters printed in newspapers or magazines.

Why did I start this chapter talking about trolling? Because you can't discuss lolcows without talking about trolls. Trolls make the lolcow.

Online trolling can take the innocuous form of posting disruptive comments and messages, and spamming. Trolls can also take things out of the digital world and into the real world. Trolls may conduct *doxxing* - where a creator's personal information like full name, address, phone number, etc. is made public. This can open a creator to harassment and unwanted contact outside of the online space. Trolls have also called into a creator's job and complained or left negative reviews for the business in an effort to get the creator fired. Using social media and other tools, trolls might contact a creator's family members or friends to harass them.

It can also escalate into more serious and criminal activity. Trolls have hacked creators' online accounts, stolen identities, and made threats of violence. Other acts, and perhaps the most infamous, are *swatting* incidents where a fake threat is called into 911, like a hostage situation, forcing law enforcement to the creator's home with guns drawn. This is often done while a creator is livestreaming, so the troll can see his handy work.

The line between trolling/tricks and illegal activity also predates the internet. Possibly the greatest troll of all time was Richard Nixon's Committee to Re-Elect the President (CREEP) in the election of 1972. They forged letters, sabotaged phone banks, disrupted rallies, and of course, broke into the Watergate Hotel to bug phones and steal documents. These dirty tricks earned Nixon the "Tricky Dick" moniker. Once they were revealed to the public, they forced him into resignation.

There is a line between trolling, practical jokes, and criticism. Practical jokes may have some level of embarrassment, frustration, or disruption. The main difference between joking and trolling is the intent of the troll vs the joker. The joker is wanting to get a laugh from everyone, including the person being pranked, and has no ill intent. The troll is there to laugh at the victim. There is no joke to be let in on.

Many negative comments might be perceived by creators as trolling but are in fact criticism. Criticism, even crude or vulgar, like a comment simply stating, "this sucks" is not intended to have ulterior motives. It is an honest opinion.

This brings us finally to the question at hand: What is a lolcow? The word lolcow is a portmanteau of "lol" - laugh out loud and "cow" - someone who is milked. A lolcow is someone baited or tricked into responding to trolls thereby "milking" them for amusing reactions. It is the troll's ultimate goal. This reaction can be the creator's shock, annoyance, or bemusement. Trolling can also be more extreme to get an angry, frustrated, or humiliating response. Not everyone that is trolled is a lolcow. And anyone on the internet can be trolled.

Even offline people can be trolled. The way you respond to a troll must be seen as funny to the troll. If you respond in an amusing way, and can be baited repeatedly into responding, you could become a lolcow.

For example, to borrow the classic "is your refrigerator running?" gag, let's say you called 100 people and ask them the question and go through the whole bit.

Some people who answer the phone will know immediately it's a troll and hang up. They are not a lolcow - they did not even hear the trolling.

Let's say you call people and go through the whole bit and the person simply replies, "my refrigerator isn't running, it's just sitting there". They aren't a lolcow. They have been trolled but they didn't react to the trolling because they did not detect or understand it. And their reaction wasn't amusing.

If you did the gag and the person replied, "Haha. Very funny," and they either legitimately thought it was funny or were indicating they understood the trolling; they aren't a lolcow either. They reacted, but they were aware of the trolling and didn't provide any negative or amusing reactions.

Imagine we reached someone, and after listening to the bit, they exploded with anger, "How dare you call me! How dare you waste my time with this call! You are tying up my phone line!" and then hung up. A troll would find it to be a very amusing reaction. Such a disproportionally high-level response to a basic troll everybody knows is amusing. For a troll, this person is a great target.

Now, let's imagine we called him the next day, and he had the same reaction - only angrier. It would be very amusing for the second time. And let's say every time we called him, say for a week straight, instead of ignoring us, he answered. And every time we called and delivered the troll line, he reacted violently and to an amusing degree. That is a lolcow. We have all three elements: the trolling, the amusing reaction to the trolling, and the milking for laughs.

Let's just say 1 in 10,000 people is susceptible to becoming a lolcow using the "is your refrigerator running?" gag. You would be dialing for a very long time before you were able to locate a lolcow. And that's assuming that person is at home at the time, heard the phone ring, and got to the phone in time. You could be dialing and calling for hundreds of hours before you found a bonafide lolcow in the wild.

The difference between calling people on a landline phone and YouTube is that there are millions of people readily available on the internet. On the internet, there are also other trolls who are active. Trolls can communicate with each other. With the power of a search engine, it's easy to locate a known lolcow and go to work.

In the landline world, it would be like if at the back of the phone book there was a list of numbers for people who got really annoyed by prank calls. Anyone wanting to make a prank call would go immediately to that section, as opposed to going through the phone book alphabetically. Today, almost all lolcows are found on the internet or by the internet, and the trolling and reaction of the lolcows are posted on the internet. Because the internet is so integral to the process of trolling and reactions, it is not necessary to distinguish between "internet lolcows" and "lolcows". Almost all lolcows are internet lolcows.

How do YouTubers become lolcows? Most lolcows fit into a pattern:

1. Initial success and high standing
2. Stale content

3. Controversy that alienates fans and co-creators
4. Refusal or inability to change and the eventual failure to deliver on promises
5. Responding to trolls (this is where lolcow status begins)
6. Ironic viewership, hate watchers, and the rise of detractors
7. Cease being known for original content (algorithm only shows detractor content)
8. Irrelevancy and subsistence living

Stage #1: Initial Success and High Standing

Most lolcows began as regular content creators. All creators have a peak. And this is not unique to YouTubers. This is true of all creators or all creative talent.

Think of any band, even if they are still alive and touring; they may be very successful and still sell shows, but they peaked in terms of sales, cultural relevancy, or artistic expression years ago. In the television world, all shows eventually have peak viewership and then fade away with time. And the show is eventually cancelled. This is even more apparent in films. Most sequels have diminishing returns. Even if films keep being made, they rarely recapture the peak of the earlier films.

And this is because the world changes. After something is created and becomes successful, it is no longer revolutionary or novel. With time, it becomes normal. The audience gets bored. Even the creator behind it might get bored. People want something different. In the YouTube space, the peak of the creator is not linear or predictable, but it does happen, and there are usually some reasons behind it.

YouTube is an ever-changing place. Algorithm shifts, moderation policies, or pressure from advertisers can disrupt a YouTubers' content. During changing political times, topics and content might become toxic or fall out of favor with advertisers resulting in an *Ad-pocalypse.* There is also changing audience taste. What was trendy years ago may be old and stale. For example, *Let's Plays,* gameplay footage overlaid with commentary, was almost entirely supplanted by live streaming.

There is also more competition now. There are more YouTube channels now than ever before. There are also other video hosting platforms like Kick, Rumble, and Bitchute. Not just from other online content creators, but more platforms like TikTok, Instagram, and Twitch. Because these creators were public figures, and rose to some level of prominence, they opened themselves up to trolling. There are very few lolcows that only have a few hundred subscribers because trolls would have a hard time finding them amongst the millions of other creators.

Stage #2: Stale Content

After the peak, stagnation follows. Stagnation can be the product of outside factors, as referenced previously, but a YouTuber who can evolve with the times and has the discipline to persevere can usually continue to grow, albeit at a slower pace. Staying relevant on YouTube becomes a marathon, and not a sprint. As some of the audience gets bored and moves on, a new audience discovering their content can be brought in.

There are underlying conditions which lead to stagnation even without the YouTuber realizing it. The first is the need for consistent uploads. The algorithm rewards this. Consistent uploads also keep your established audience engaged and keep your videos at the top of their subscribers list. However, these consistent uploads keep YouTubers making videos of subpar quality just to keep up with demand. A YouTuber might run out of ideas, or an idea may not be good enough for a video. *But they need to put a video out.* The constant need for uploads can cause a creator to get comfortable, or see it as acceptable, to pump out mediocre content.

The second is the streamlined creation process. Due to the demand of the algorithm, it becomes expedient for a YouTuber to have an assembly line like process for content creation. Like an assembly line, this established process creates standardization and efficiency. *Standardization* and *efficiency* don't sound very *artistic* and *creative*. An artist who creates every painting from scratch, and each painting is a new canvas, has a lot more weight than an artist printing a lot of posters. Once the content assembly line is complete and put into motion, each video starts to become exactly like the last one. This stagnates creativity, the artistic expression, and (most importantly) the entertainment value of their videos.

The third factor is the general decline in ambition and drive to continue. After scrimping and clawing their way to the top, they begin to enjoy the fruit of their labor. If they are financially successful, content creation went from necessity of survival to hobby. This is not a phenomenon unique to YouTubers. For example, great boxers and MMA fighters, after becoming the champion and making millions of dollars, no longer feel it is necessary to get beat up anymore. Dana White, head of the UFC once said, "Once the money starts to pile up … Getting punched in the face every day isn't too f**king cool. They reach financial security, or once they feel they have financial security, the toll [physical damage, risk] becomes less acceptable." (Samuelson, 2012)

There is a grind when it comes to running a YouTube channel. It is not like a TV show where it has seasons of production. A band might go on tour, but that lasts a few months at a time, and then there is some respite. Other media where a performer may have to do a show every day, like a game show host or late-night host, have a staff of writers and producers to assist them. A YouTuber is a mainly solitary enterprise where they are the main creative force behind the channel, and any staff are auxiliary.

After content stagnation is a decline of viewership, subscribers, and engagement. Usually, the first to decline is viewership. People aren't watching. Why aren't people watching the videos anymore? The simple answer is: their content is not entertaining.

The second metric to decline is engagement. This engagement would be likes, chats/super chats, and comments. It is still possible to maintain the same level of engagement, with falling viewers, if you have a dedicated fan base.

The third metric to decline is subscribers. This is usually the last to decline because most people don't go through the effort of unsubscribing from a channel. They simply stop watching. Periodic purges of inactive or bot accounts and other attrition will slowly drain a subscriber count.

Many creators might assume this decline is due to factors outside of their control. This can be seen as a "mental cope" by the struggling creator. But sometimes these are factual. For example, if you make political content, there is an increase in traffic during the election cycle and decrease after the election. This is also seen in non-internet media as well. If you make sports content, like football, in the offseason a YouTuber will see a decline because the playing season is over. If you made gardening videos, these declines might be *literally seasonal* as your content slows down outside of the growing season. But these declines are just seasonal adjustments. For example, retailers don't expect the Christmas holiday sales numbers to keep going up through January and February. They are seasonal if they can be charted and happen regularly. Many YouTubers' content is not seasonal, and they are often in denial until it is clearly demonstrated the long-term trend is downward.

The creator is usually acutely aware of this decline or *reverse growth* since YouTube provides creators with analytics. There are also third-party sites like SocialBlade that can be used to view this as well. Outside of any metrics, the financial decline will surely be noticed. This feeling of peaking or declining may trigger a sunsetting malaise. The peak or decline will often be referenced by the YouTuber and the insecurity about being a "has been" may feed additional trolling.

Stage #3: Controversy that Alienates Fans and Co-Creators

All public figures have some degree of controversy which erupts around them at some point in their career. Sometimes controversies are trivial and blow over quickly. Other controversies can destroy your career. I'm not going to get into the controversies themselves, but how people deal with controversy.

Only successful YouTubers have controversies. A YouTuber with 300 subscribers is not going to have a controversy everyone is talking about. Just like your average Joe getting a DUI doesn't make local news, but a Hollywood celebrity getting a DUI would make national headlines.

A controversy is bound to lead to some people leaving or not watching anymore. It is true "the internet never forgets" but it is also true "the internet doesn't remember things for long". A growing YouTuber can replace an audience that is leaving with a new audience. The issue arises when the channel is no longer growing. The audience is leaving, but nobody is coming in and replacing them.

YouTubers face controversy all the time. In fact, YouTubers might seek out controversy for clicks and views. YouTubers might even become accustomed to controversy as a way of growing the channel. Inserting yourself in controversies works in a creator's *growth* stage. You can grab attention and stand out from the crowd. But there is a difference between seeking out controversy, and inserting yourself to get attention, and becoming the controversy where you are a target.

The other issue that controversy creates a *feeding frenzy* around successful YouTubers. There are hundreds or thousands of medium sized (100,000 to 500,000 subscribers) YouTubers competing in whatever genre they cater to. If a large YouTuber (1,000,000+ subscribers) has a controversy, all the attention from all smaller creators will be focused on the larger creator. It will be one hundred small voices against one large voice. This negative attention can push the target creator out of the algorithm to the point were searching that YouTuber's name won't bring up their channel, but tons of negative videos of people operating in the same space as them.

This feeding frenzy also turns off other creators that may have previously collaborated with the large successful YouTuber. Generally, larger channels are in a position of power, and smaller channels will try to collaborate to gain cross pollination from the larger creator's audience. As controversies occur, there is a natural attrition rate of abandonment of once-friendly collaborators.

In fact, the incentives are for smaller channels to turn against the larger channel. If the audience leaves the larger channel, they won't stop being interested in the genre; they just switch to the smaller channel. For example, if Ford is making a Pinto that kills people, people don't stop buying cars. They simply switch to a Ford competitor, like Toyota.

There are three main ways people deal with controversy: address it directly, deflect, or silence. And these strategies must also be made within a certain time frame to have the intended effect.

Addressing it directly must be done quickly and promptly for it to have any effect. A public statement is sent out that either apologizes, reframes, downplays, or explains their side of the story to try to add context.

Deflection is usually when the public figure doesn't address the matter directly, but when asked about it will respond. Usually, the response is to downplay the controversy or bring up other examples where there was no controversy.

Silence or laying low is just that, not addressing it and even departing from the public eye for a while. The news cycle changes, the media moves on, and then the public figure can re-emerge once the controversy blows over.

The problem for YouTubers is that some of these are not viable options. Silence is a difficult option because the whole purpose of a YouTuber is to "Broadcast Yourself". YouTubers are not like Hollywood celebrities, who can go months at a time without appearing in public. Constant uploads are necessary to remain relevant and are built into a YouTuber's routine. Not posting videos also creates a financial strain from lost revenue. Waiting for the controversy to blow over might take months, which is an eternity in YouTube time. By the time they return, the algorithm, the audience, and subscribers may have already moved onto other channels.

Deflection is less difficult but precarious. Because the YouTuber can receive constant communication from the audience, the audience may keep pestering them regarding the controversy. YouTubers can receive super chats and their comments sections can be filled with constant discussion about how they are not addressing the controversy. It can be dragged out for months because they could respond to the controversy but did not address it.

For example, other public figures might make a statement, use deflection, and then go about their business. Again, keeping with the Hollywood celebrity example, they might do an interview, post a video or press conference, and deflect. They can choose not to engage with the media. They will most likely never be pressed on that controversy for quite some time. Given time, the controversy will have blown over.

But because the YouTuber must keep uploading and is constantly facing the audience, addressing the controversy is usually what they choose. YouTubers can also double down in addressing the controversy. Someone standing up for themselves can appeal to supporters and quash a *non-troversy*.

It's an understood cliche to come out with an "apology video" where the creator explains why they were wrong and strives to do better. This happens so frequently because it can be the best option. It placates the aggressive hawks on the controversy that are pressing the topic and squashes the controversy by not allowing it to linger on. The apology video can be the least bad option. The only problem with the apology video is it puts the YouTuber on record as trying to change and relies on the audience to hold them accountable.

Stage #4: Refusal or Inability to Change and The Eventual Failure to Deliver on Promises

At this stage in the YouTuber's career, they are at a crossroads. And it is not too late to reverse course. They have peaked, stagnated, are possibly in decline, and are being targeted by real or trumped-up controversies. This is also the last stop on the way to being a lolcow.

What is needed to turn things around at this point? On a human level, reinvigoration is needed. Maybe take time away from the internet. Maybe touch grass. From a channel perspective, content evolution is needed. There must be some creative influx to change things up. Focus on quality. Move away from, or setup a new, content assembly line.

The problem with changing is that it requires the conscientiousness to recognize the present course is untenable AND the discipline and will to enact change. This is not just true for YouTubers but for people in general. Why do people not have the ability to change? People get stuck in their comfort zone and habits. There is a fear of change; that is really a fear of the unknown or failure. There are social, environmental, or cultural pressures which reinforce current behaviors. Others might want to change but lack the tools or support system to do so. And some people might have biological factors like stress, depression, and addiction which make it difficult to change.

Once a YouTuber is aware they are stagnating or in decline (assuming they are not in denial), there must be a self-reflection that the course they are on is untenable. And many YouTubers know this. They might even make updates to their channel and talk about how things are slowing down. They may make promises to improve content, deliver more content, or make new content.

The best-case scenario is that these promises of change have a follow-through that will reverse negative growth and put the YouTuber back on the path to positive growth. Though this is just the cycle repeating - growth, peak, stagnation, decline. In the long run, they will reach another peak and face the same issue. But successful YouTubers are able to change and evolve with the times and stay relevant. YouTubing is a marathon, not a sprint.

Lolcows don't have the conscientiousness and/or discipline to change. And because they refuse to change or have some inability to change, they stay on the downward trajectory. In most cases, they only go through one cycle. The first time they get to the stagnation and decline stage, they cannot reverse the trend and continue downwards.

Stage #5: Responding to Trolls

Responding to trolls is the first step in becoming a lolcow. Every YouTuber has trolls, and trolling has been going on at every stage of the YouTuber's cycle: growth, peak, stagnation, and decline. Even during a YouTuber's growth and peak stages, they may have been responding to trolls. However, at these early stages, their strong position and audience growth can mask the damage responding to trolls can cause.

When it comes to trolls, the only winning move is not to play. The whole point of trolling to receive a reaction. The more a YouTuber reacts, the more the troll wins. And usually the fiercer the reaction, the more amusing the trolls find it. The more amusing the trolls find it, the more they will troll.

Why would someone react to a troll? It could be argued responding to trolls is instinctual. Defending yourself from attacks is the natural response. For a regular person, it can be very easy to get sucked into one of these encounters. A regular person doesn't have the knowledge or discipline that comes with being a public figure. The real question is, why would a creator/YouTuber/public figure react to a troll? They are supposed to understand how the internet works. That's how they reached their position of success in the first place.

The answer to that is very complicated, and we will cover that in subsequent chapters. But as far as the stages of the lolcow, you must put yourself in the position of the creator at this stage in the cycle. They have experienced their peak - usually some kind of notoriety and success. They have stagnated. Fans are leaving. Other creators, who may have "collaborated" with them (the closest thing a YouTuber has to a co-worker) are distancing themselves. The decline in viewership and engagement may also be negatively impacting the creator financially. This creates financial stress. There is also the psychological stress of falling behind or fading relevancy. All these stressors *combined* might make someone susceptible, letting their guard down, and responding to the trolls.

By responding to trolls, it distracts from the actual content the creator is trying to provide to the audience. Instead of the show being about entertaining the audience, the show becomes the creator responding to trolls. This distraction is not just the time spent in videos, but vampirically saps the YouTuber's time and creative energy. Responding to the trolls becomes the "content". If not handled quickly, this becomes a doom loop. This negative spiral: shrinking audience > creator's stress > responding to trolls > stale content > shrinking audience - can become the state of mind of the creator. This negative headspace drives lolcow behavior and further escalates the stages of lolcowdom.

Stage #6: Ironic Viewership, Hate Watchers, and Rise of Detractors

Most of the regular audience of the creator has stopped watching at this point, but that doesn't mean there is no audience. There is a subculture of people online called *detractors* who watch the subject creator ironically or *hate watch*. Hate watching is consuming content, not because it is enjoyable, but because they dislike it. The "entertainment" comes from mocking it, picking it apart, or reveling in the dislike for it. This hate watching may even provide the creator with an increase in viewership. However, any increase in detractors watching your content is not a positive development in the long run. It should be a signal to a creator that their YouTube career is not sustainable. It is very difficult to monetize people disliking your content instead of organically supporting it.

Who are these detractors? Many of these detractors were prior fans of the subject creator. They might feel the creator betrayed themselves or their fans. Many have a personal reason to dislike or revulsion to the subject creator. Many also think of themselves as internet archivists/historians who want to set the record straight and "highlight" the truth by creating detractor content. Others just find lolcows to be subjects of amusement and wish to point and laugh. They may also publish content so that others can laugh with them.

Once there is an appetite for hate watching, there are detractor channels that rise up to cater to this new detractor audience. Detractors and detractor content may also conduct *a-logging*. A-logging comes from Anthony Logatto, a member of the Sonichu/Chris Chan online community who made constant, aggressive rants about Chris Chan. And the term *logging* is also a computer term for archiving. Many a-logs are fixated on criticizing a creator. This fixation includes going through backlogs of the creator's content to identify embarrassing or suspect material that gets lost in the thousands of hours of content. This cataloguing of "lowlights" (instead of highlights) is meant for the purposes of laughing or criticizing the subject creator.

For example, there could be a detractor channel focused on a creator who streams video games. A detractor might make a compilation of the subject creator dying in the game repeatedly. They could take a long live stream and engage in *clipping* - and focus in on the subject creator's confusion/frustration at the game mechanics. All of this would serve the detractor channel's purpose by creating an indictment of the subject creator's gaming skills. The detractor audience then watches these videos.

Online detractors are different from trolls, even if a creator may lump them together. Detractor content, or detractors, catalogue or document other creators, usually for the purposes of amusement and criticism. They are different from trolls because detractors don't make content for the purposes of getting a reaction from the creator. Detractors may not even interact with their target creator at all. Detractor content stands on its own. Their criticism is their form of content/entertainment. A creator may react to detractor content, and the detractor may even want a creator to watch it, but the intent and purpose is to create new content. The detractor's target is merely the subject of that new content.

The difference between a detractor and a critic is that the critic is focusing on the subject with positives and negatives. For example, a film critic watches movies and gives the film criticism. And the critic talks about the good and bad parts of the film and usually recommends or does not recommend seeing it. A critic's value is helping the public spend our limited time and money on good movies and avoid bad movies. Detractors almost exclusively focus on the negative of the subject. They don't exist to compare the subject (the target YouTuber) to other subjects.

If a creator is so bad they have detractor channels rise up and gain traction online, combined with their own stagnating or falling viewership, it may bring the detractor channel the same recognition as the original creator's channel. People, over time, learn about the creator not through their own channel, but through the detractor's channel. And come to know the creator through the lens of a detractor.

As the creator gains infamy from this detractor content, many of the new people being introduced to their content become trolls. And if the creator is continually responding to trolling, this creates a negative feedback loop: trolling occurs > reaction from creator > reaction provides entertaining detractor content > detractor channel grows > more people watch detractor content > trolling occurs.

Stage #7: Cease Being Known for Their Own Content

As the creator's original content declines in popularity and the detractor content grows in popularity, the YouTube algorithm will no longer take you to the original creator.

If you search a non-lolcow creator into YouTube, generally their channel and their videos will be in the top ten results. If you search a lolcow creator into YouTube, you will be flooded by detractor content and *maybe* one of the results will be of the original creator.

This is a sign there is not enough actual organic support and viewership to have a sustainable YouTube career.

Because it is nearly impossible to find any of the original content beset by all the detractor content, it is impossible to grow the creator's channel. You can't grow a channel with detractors. At this point in time, the creator has become a lolcow and their YouTube career is effectively over.

Stage #8: Irrelevancy and Subsistence Living

Even though their career is effectively over, the lolcow may soldier on creating content. This is also the point where lolcows begin to request financial support or engage in *e-begging*. E-begging is when someone is asking for financial support over the internet. The lolcow's growing financial desperation is mentioned more and more in videos. Some will even make it the subject of content in a vain attempt to gain sympathy or misguided effort to make content. This insecurity, which is broadcast by the creator, is also usually the target of trolling and detractor content.

If the creator was very successful, they could still be making revenue from their enormous back catalogue of videos. However, there is a very small amount of money to be made from this. The remaining financial support mainly comes from holdout fans, sympathy supporters, and the trolls/detractors themselves.

Holdout fans are the most dedicated and loyal fans. Despite the decline in content quality, controversy, trolling, and detractors they still watch and enjoy the content unironically. They may have been with the creator for years and still support the channel. Let's say a channel which used to bring in 1,000 people on a livestream brings in 90% less viewership, that would still net the creator 100 viewers. The more successful a creator was originally, generally the more hold out fans still exist.

Sympathy supporters are people who feel bad for the creator because of the trolling and detractor content. They may believe that the creator's diminished financial position is not because of the creator's bad content or bad choices, but due to the trolling/detractor content. Out of sympathy, they will provide some financial assistance, not because they find the content entertaining.

Among these holdout fans and sympathy supporters are *whales*. The concept of whales predates the internet. In a gambling context, whales are the people who spend disproportionally large amounts of money at the casino. Most people might go to a casino and drop $20 into the penny slots, play a few hands of blackjack, or a small bet on their favorite sports team. Whales spend thousands of dollars at the casino. And the casino rewards them with perks, like free rooms or rewards programs, to keep them coming back. In the online world, a few big whales can keep a creator afloat. Whereas a regular super chat or donation might be a few dollars ($1 to $5) to a creator occasionally, whales regularly give disproportionately high donations, memberships, or gifts. What are the perks of being a whale to an online creator? You get a response from the creator. Just like a troll's urge to get a response from a creator, some people (for whatever reason), want some special recognition from someone they think is important.

Trolls and detractors could, surprisingly, become a means of financial support to the lolcow. Trolls use the "super chat" function to coax the creator into responding to insults or other verbal abuses. Trolls may pay for the creator to perform humiliation rituals on camera for them to laugh at. Detractors might pay the creator to avoid the subject creator flagging or issuing copyright takedowns of their detractor videos.

The problem is even if you scrape all ad venues from past successful videos, whale donations, and troll money, it doesn't hold a candle to a creator's earnings when they were at the growth or peak stage of their career. Most lolcows barely scrape by earning a poor to working class wage. To my knowledge, there are no lolcows who are making as much money as compared to when they were in their successful growing phase. Why do these lolcows persist in content creation when there is little financial incentive? I will cover that in a future chapters.

Chapter 3: How the Internet Birthed Lolcows

Lolcows are very rare outside of the internet because online content creators are a unique kind of public figure. When I pondered the question, "how did lolcows get started?" or "why do lolcows exist on the internet?", it brought me back to the question of: "why *aren't* there lolcows in other forms of media?" There must be unique qualities of the internet and online content creation which allow for the emergence of lolcows.

We have to go back to the very definition of a lolcow: someone baited or tricked into responding to trolls thereby "milking" them for amusing reactions. For the lolcow to exist, there must be 4 conditions:

> 1. People who are susceptible to trolling are public figures - that way they can be found by trolls.
> 2. People susceptible to trolling must be able to receive the trolling.
> 3. The trolled person must be able to react to the troll.
> 4. The person's reaction to the troll must be seen by the public and the troll.

Being a public figure requires prudence to navigate and weather the storms of public life. Why don't lolcows exhibit prudence? I believe it is due to the process of creation without checks, immediate feedback from the audience, and the role of the internet itself.

The Prudence of a Public Figure

People become public figures as a natural consequence of the employment they choose. The degree of "public" depends on how much a person puts themselves into the public eye. For example, lawyers who advertise become recognizable from their billboards or television ads. They are recognizable to the public. Those same people wouldn't be able to pick out their county's district attorney. People may know Steve Jobs or Bill Gates, but other tech icons who were just as important to the development of technology, like Steve Wozniak or Paul Allen, could be unknown to most people because they had lower public profiles.

Prudence is the ability to think carefully before acting, foresee possible outcomes, and choose the best course of action. Everyone exercises prudence in their daily life. Humans are a social species. We have certain cultural norms that must be observed to be a functioning member of that society. And it is especially important as a public figure, who has a high social status, to carefully navigate social situations to maintain that status. They take actions to enhance their social status and avoid actions which would hurt their status.

Damage to your reputation can undermine or destroy a public figure. This is especially true in the entertainment industry. Prudence to avoid these social mistakes and prudence on how to deal with the fallout of these mistakes can make or break your career.

Lolcows either don't have a conception of themselves as public figures or do not exercise prudence when dealing with the public.

No Gatekeeping Online

Having no gatekeeping presents unique opportunities but also unique issues. One of the biggest advantages is that it is open to everyone. One of the biggest issues is that it is open to everyone. People who are not suited to the role join the industry.

I've never seen a band get on stage where every instrument is out of tune. It would never happen. You couldn't buy tickets to a show like that even if you wanted to. I've also never bought a book at the store where there were multiple misspellings and blatantly incorrect grammar.

Why have we never seen these things? Because there are gatekeepers along the way to stop these things from happening. There are countless people with delusions of grandeur that they are some great singer. *American Idol* has found many of them and put them on public display for people to laugh at. There are always authors who think they have revolutionary ideas or great stories but are confusing muddled messes of words strung together.

The reason these "creators" never reach millions of people is because someone has rejected them. The band that sings offkey didn't get an audition from the record company. The author who doesn't know how to spell couldn't get representation with a literary agent. They were all turned away by the gatekeepers. So, when we see a bad band, or read a boring book, that was the stuff that got past the gatekeepers.

Compare the gatekeeping process of other forms of media to the YouTube videos published and available for millions of people. Imagine for a moment a world in which an author could sit down at his word processor and complete a book. It's saved on the computer. In a few short clicks, he can take that work and put it in every library and bookstore in the world. His book is now right next to best-selling authors. This is the power of YouTube.

Even if creators were not outright rejected by gatekeepers, there are other checks and balances which prevent the "really bad stuff" from getting through. Many different people who contribute to a project polish the work to make it better. The reason why we rarely find spelling errors in books is because an agent, at least one editor, and a publisher have gone through it and found them. Even the most experienced author, with spell check, and after reading it several times, might miss something. Even for a short book, there might be dozens of drafts which get corrected and edited. More people go through the work, and those mistakes are removed by the time the book is published.

Because there were checks and balances through different stages of production, many creators are rejected outright, and the ones who make it through are constantly corrected through a process of review. Something totally unpolished would never go out the door and reach a consumer because someone along the way would have stepped in and either fixed it or told the person they have no talent and give it up.

Additionally, rejection or editing is not the end of a creator's journey. Many famous and successful creators were rejected many times. This initial rejection hardened their resolve. And many rejections don't come with just a flat "no". Many people offer constructive criticism along the way. Rejection and criticism increased their mental toughness and helped them refine their skills.

Even creators who have had early success have been rejected. For example, J.K. Rowling, whose first published book *Harry Potter and the Philosopher's Stone*, was a best seller - it was still rejected by seven publishers. Many creators have early projects that went nowhere. Think of the most famous musicians, many did not become famous as part of their first band. John Lennon and Paul McCartney didn't start with *The Beatles;* they started with *The Quarrymen.*

For YouTubers, it is a profession open to anybody. There are no gatekeepers, no rejection, and no polishing or editing by producers. YouTubers are isolated from these rejections because they work totally independently of any oversight. Just because you *can* do something doesn't mean you *should* do something.

Creation without Checks (or Balances)

In any creative endeavor, there is some degree of collaboration. Some sort of checks and balances system which moderates, regulates, and revises the end creative product and *the people* who work within the creative system.

The largest scale artistic endeavors we have in modern society are films. The largest films cost nearly a billion dollars. Even small independent films cost millions of dollars. You need actors, animators, effects, cinematographers, costume and prop specialists, musicians, editors, producers, the director, and many others. The most powerful man that works creatively behind a movie project is the director.

The director is the head of this massive operation, but even the power of the director, despite the massive resources of a large Hollywood production, is also limited by his interactions, inputs, suggestions, and orders from everyone that he works with. Even the director has some other person who is financially backing him. The director answers to the producer/studio who hired him. The director may approve certain elements of a film or change things, but many aspects of the film or final product he did not "directly" involve himself in. Many directors don't write their own scores, stitch their own costumes together, or build their own sets. This constant interaction, management of resources, and working with people means directors must be regulated in their actions and interactions.

This constant communication and interlocking checks and balances on the director and his artistic vision, forces the director to refine and modify his vision. Outside financial constraints compel him to complete the movie. The director's abilities are also constantly being put to the test. If a director fails, or the movie doesn't make money, they are fired by the studio. Just to be a director, at any level, requires skill and a body of work to prepare him for that job.

A smaller scale creative endeavor would be a music band. A small group of people, often even high schoolers, is all that is needed to form a band. With the limited resources of a few amps and instruments, young bands try to strike it big. Within the band itself, there is some degree of specialization and differing talent levels. Some members write, some play an instrument, some sing, and some do all three. While it is possible to handle all aspects of the band in-house, the most successful bands have sound technicians, marketing managers, merchandise managers, producers, etc. Most bands usually sign with a record label who provides them with these resources. Most successful independent musicians were previously signed by labels; only after fame and fortune do they have the financial stability to be unsigned. In fact, many aspiring artists are hopeful to sign a record deal, like a small startup company looks forward to getting institutional investor support. These record companies manage the band, adding checks and balances.

On the other end of the spectrum, a more isolated creative endeavor would be writing. When you write a book, it can be near solitary activity. But even authors have agents, editors, and publishers who review the final work before it is published.

In film making, music production, or authoring a book, there are always multiple layers the director, musician, or author must go through for their product to reach an audience. And in cases where they don't go through layers, they are only able to reach a niche audience. Authors may self-publish, which is very much like someone posting on YouTube, but a self-published book very rarely ends up being a best seller or receiving any attention outside of a niche audience. Musicians might perform on the sidewalk, but only a few hundred people would ever hear them.

Unlike other forms of media, YouTube has two distinct differences: 1) there is no gatekeeping on who can make content and 2) anyone can start and deliver a product with a totally vertically integrated production to publishing model AND reach millions of people.

The only gatekeeping to becoming a YouTuber is technological. You need a computer, an email, a YouTube account, an internet connection, and be 18 years old or have guardian permission - that's it. Most people on planet Earth today have or can obtain the ability to publish YouTube videos. Just because it is possible to do it, doesn't mean that people should do it - as Ian Malcom reminded us in *Jurassic Park*. Many people not suitable, because of bad temperament, lack of talent, or poor discipline, who would normally get weeded out (in other forms of media) – can become successful on YouTube.

The Role of The Internet Itself

Because lolcows are living, breathing people, there are real world forces that act upon them. These real-world forces affect you and me just as much as the lolcows: the economy, government policy, technology, war, car accidents, health diagnosis, etc. For an online creator, the biggest real-world force in their life is the internet.

We spend so much time discussing how online creators put their mark on the internet. What about the mark the internet leaves on the creator? The internet is a two-way system. Internet usage is normal. But being "terminally online" and spending most of your time on the internet has *real* health risks. Those risks are well documented in many medical and psychological studies. Spending too much time online has mental health, physical health, and social/lifestyle risks.

I would argue being "online" is a constant for online creators and YouTubers. Constant exposure to news, trolling, drama, and negative content can be harmful. Social media and gaming platforms are designed to reward compulsive use (likes, comments, notifications). Heavy exposure to extremist forums, conspiracy content, or toxic communities can skew one's perception of reality. *Main character syndrome,* the feeling every online event is about you, distorts your reality.

Hours of sitting lead to increased risk of obesity, cardiovascular disease, diabetes, and premature mortality. People heavily online may skip meals, snack excessively, or eat mostly junk food, impacting long-term health. There are additional long-term risks like reduced attention span, poorer memory, and difficulty with focus.

Online interactions can displace in-person relationships, leaving people socially disconnected despite being "always connected." Being deeply engaged in online arguments or communities (especially toxic ones) can cause stress. It could impact your self-esteem if your self-worth becomes tied to online validation. There is also significant opportunity cost. Time spent excessively online is time not spent on career, hobbies, education, or personal growth. This opportunity cost can destroy, or severely limit, a creator's offline world.

Receiving the Trolling

People who are susceptible to trolling become public figures as online content creators because there are no gatekeepers, no checks and balances in the creation process, and being terminally online distorts your faculties. There must now be a mechanism for the susceptible person to receive the trolling.

The connectivity of the internet is the missing piece other forms of media don't have. The internet is not just a broadcast transmission, but also a receiver of information. And the audience can react in real time to the creator.

What makes the internet different from other forms of live media? For example, an audience can react to a play in a theater in real time. There are several distinct differences between being in a theater and being online. The first is that physical presence is necessary. The second is that your physical presence exists in a moderated space - the theater. If you are disruptive during the performance, the theater manager can throw you out. Nobody can throw you off the internet. The third is that you paid for a ticket. You have a "buy in" so to speak. If you are disruptive, and thrown out, you would lose the price of admission. There is a cost to trolling in real life. The fourth is that you don't have anonymity in the real world. If you cause issues for the play, in the theater, you can face real world consequences, like getting arrested.

The internet has the exact opposite on all four points: virtual presence only, there is no moderated space, it's free, and there is almost complete anonymity online. The risk and cost of trolling is *zero*.

The internet also makes sending trolling very easy. How could you get a public figure's attention before the internet? If you aren't physically in front of them, it's very difficult. You could write them a letter or try to reach them by phone. Those were the only options available back then.

On the internet, trolls can send the creator super chats that they either have to read or acknowledge. Creators are also active on social media. Trolls can find them on social media and message them. If they are streaming video games, they can join the lobby of the said game to troll them. There is a constant "chat" active during livestreams. Have you ever watched CNBC or some other news channel and they have the ticker running at the bottom of the screen? It's a natural human tendency to read that. It's the same with chat. Creators try to respond to chat to drive engagement.

Broadcasting the Reaction to Trolling

The reaction to the trolling must make its way back to the troll. This is their amusement. Trolling someone and not being able to see their reaction makes it much less interesting. The internet makes this broadcasting of "reaction" possible. Broadcasting also allows for spectators of trolling.

For example, let's think back to pre-internet trolling. Anybody can leave anybody else a wacky voicemail. It could be something strange, vulgar, or funny. It's a harmless, practical joke. But the troll can't see the reaction. On the internet, you can super chat someone something strange, vulgar, or funny and the creator reacts in real time.

There are other creative forms of trolling using the internet. For example, sending the creator items via DoorDash or UberEats. The DoorDash arrives on stream, forcing the creator to answer the door. They then open the box and find something amusing like cucumbers and condoms or something. Even if the creator doesn't answer the door, simply acting annoyed at someone knocking on the door could be enough for a troll.

Chapter 4: Traits of the Lolcow

To identify anything, you must understand the traits of something. In my study of lolcows, I have identified ten traits most lolcows share:

1. Parasocial relationship with the audience
2. Content is generally accepted as bad
3. Currently self-employed, previously held a menial job
4. Reviled or infamous for repugnant behavior
5. Universally mocked or ridiculed
6. Oversharing personal information
7. Personality flaws
8. Unable to build a new audience or reinvent themselves
9. Financial desperation or dire straits
10. Inability to quit being a public figure

Trait # 1: Parasocial Relationship with the Audience

Even before the lolcow status, lolcows exhibit an unhealthy parasocial relationship with the audience in their growth and peak states. As we will discuss in later chapters, the lolcows treat the audience as a surrogate friend. They share their embarrassing insecurities, seek unhealthy validation, and rely on financial support from this "surrogate friend".

Trait #2: Bad Content

All lolcows create bad content that can only be enjoyed ironically because it is lazy, stale, or boring. However, just because someone is making "bad" content doesn't mean they are a lolcow. "Bad" content can still get millions of views and be very monetizable.

Something that is "good" or "bad" can be subjective. But even something subjective can be judged on criteria. This is how scoring works in gymnastics, diving, and combat sports. The audience is the judge. They get to decide what is good or bad content.

While others may subjectively judge content as good or bad, each individual viewer can tell objectively whether they were entertained or not by the content. Viewers objectively choose one channel to watch over a different channel. Viewers objectively evaluate what content is not worth their time and choose to click on something else to watch. And viewers objectively decide to stop watching once it becomes boring.

Trait # 3: Currently Self Employed, Previously Held a Menial Job

Common sense would dictate with their dwindling financial prospects on the internet a lolcow would get an additional job, even a part-time job, to supplement their income. The only lolcows who have gotten jobs have been totally deplatformed.

There are many mental barriers lolcows have which prevent them from seeking employment. All these mental barriers are defense mechanisms or "excuses" lolcows deploy. We shall examine them in detail:

1. No employer will hire them because of their internet past
2. They can revive their online career
3. Inability to come to terms with becoming a "normal" person again.

4. Trolls will get them fired from any prospective job.

Lolcows often share a belief no employer will hire them because of their internet past. There is some debate, depending on the lolcow, whether they truly believe this or not. There are plenty of people with an infamous past who have jobs. There are convicted felons with jobs. They have done way worse than any online creator. Any job open to a convicted felon is open to a YouTuber. However, most of those jobs are rough, physically difficult, and low paying. Someone from a white-collar background, like online content creation, would not gravitate towards those jobs.

Lolcows mistakenly believe they can revive their online career. Many may recognize they are in decline. In fact, many use their decline for sympathy or attention. However, none of them have the correct diagnosis of why their online career is failing. This incorrect diagnosis is driven by many factors, including Trait #7 - Personality Flaws. The bottom line is that their content is bad. But most focus on blaming trolling, detractors, or other outside forces, like the YouTube algorithm.

Lolcows usually have delusions of grandeur or fatal pride which prevents them from going back to working a normal job. This is sometimes directly referenced by the lolcow. They believe being a YouTuber is a more prestigious career. They mistakenly cling to it for relevancy. This can also be related to their past holding menial jobs and not wanting to go back to that life. Offline, they would be a nobody who works behind the parts counter at AutoZone or works the Wendy's drive thru. But online, they are this famous person.

Lolcows often believe there is no point in getting a job because trolls will get them fired from said job. It is true some lolcows have "attempted" other employment, but they self-sabotage by oversharing that information (see Trait #6 -

Oversharing) and trolls contact this prospective employer. This trouble can get them fired. It is unknown whether they overshare the employer's information because that is their natural tendency OR do they have ulterior motives like, having an excuse for not working or for the purposes of pity.

In my study of lolcows, it is also surprising that many of them worked menial jobs prior to becoming a YouTuber. I don't mean they worked at McDonalds as a teenager and a menial job was a long time ago. They were working menial jobs immediately prior to becoming a YouTuber. YouTuber is a job that is open to everyone.

How did people who were unsuccessful offline gain success online? It is almost paradoxical because many of the traits necessary for becoming a successful YouTuber like hard work, creativity, self-starter, and ability to communicate are also necessary for having a successful offline career.

I would argue it is because their online success could be attributed to outside factors other than their content. For example, they had a first mover advantage in a new genre. Most of their success was based on their public persona. This persona is an artificial construction. Anyone can have a persona that is entertaining or interesting.

We will also discuss later how this history of working menial jobs did not prepare them for the complexities of being a public figure and content creator.

Trait #4: Reviled or Infamous for Repugnant Behavior

Everyone has moments in life they are not proud of. However, our worst moments weren't memorialized on the internet forever like these lolcows. Everyone has outbursts of anger, said something they regretted, or acted in disregard for others. It is a natural occurrence, and a normal person can admit they are wrong, apologize to the other party, and make a good faith effort to change for the positive.

What are some examples of the repugnant behavior which makes the lolcows infamous? This behavior exists on a sliding scale with degrees of bad. The lolcow's bad behavior intersects with ethics, overall societal/internet norms, and criminal behavior. This bad behavior can be online or offline behavior.

- Ethics: lying, hypocrisy, rug pulling, failure to deliver promises
- Breaching internet norms: engaging in doxxing, leaking private messages
- Criminal Behavior: stealing, child abuse, animal abuse, drug/alcohol addiction, assault

People who engage in bad behavior get the most negative attention. It is a self-selecting process. This bad behavior also fuels trolls and detractors with some degree of righteousness. We will explore the repugnant behavior of the lolcows in later chapters.

Trait #5: Universally Mocked or Ridiculed

It may go without saying that the "lol" in lolcow is for people laughing at them. What I want to stress in this section is the universality of their ridicule.

Before they were a lolcow, the creator enjoyed certain fame and prestige. Generally, they have online friends and allies who they share mutual interest or a mutual audience. They collaborate, which is great for content. Cross pollination between creators helps everyone grow their channel.

However, as part of spiraling into lolcow status, lolcows isolate themselves from possible support due to their toxicity. Because lolcows don't have online friends or allies, there are no voices online to come to their defense. The algorithm and public consensus turn only negative attention towards them.

Trait #6 Oversharing Personal Information

It is universally understood that based on the context of a certain kind of social interaction, there are degrees of personal information which can be shared safely. The danger of oversharing information is that information could be weaponized against you. For example, everyone has been at the check-out counter and the cashier asks, "how are you today?". It is universally understood they are not genuinely interested in your day. The customer doesn't have any social, business, or established relationship with the cashier (exception being for repeat customers). The cashier is making polite idle conversation. It would therefore be inappropriate for someone to respond how they really feel: *I fear my kid is being bullied in school, and I don't know how to help them. I don't feel fulfilled at work. My father has cancer and I can't spend enough time with him until it is too late. Etc.*

Online content creators are public figures. And public figures must be even more careful to protect their personal information. Because this is understood as common sense, I will focus on how this applies to lolcows. Why do lolcows overshare information? These fit into three main categories: psychological, social, and situational.

Psychological reasons we will explore in the section on Trait #7 - Personality Flaws. Those include the need for validation, impulse control, ego, and attention seeking.

The main social reason would be to build a connection with the audience. During the growth phase of a creator, sharing personal information can be a way to gain trust and closeness with strangers online. It can turn casual viewers into loyal supporters.

Situational reasons would be loneliness, alcohol/drug use, and stress. Content creation is a lonely endeavor. Seeking a relationship, a creator reaches out to the viewer. The relationship and parasocial relationship between a viewer and creator can sometimes be inverted, and the creator is using the audience as a surrogate friend. In doing so, they mistakenly entrust this surrogate friend with sensitive personal information.

Many YouTubers engage in drinking or drug use while on stream. It's well documented that other creators like musicians and actors engage in alcohol/drug use to cope with the isolation and pressure of being a public performer. Many creators may mistakenly believe that "loosening up" with inhibition-suppressing substances increases their artistic expression or improves entertainment. However, because the YouTuber is now uninhibited, they are much more likely to engage in oversharing.

The stress of being a public figure, content creation, fame, financial distress etc. eats away at the YouTuber and in a moment of weakness they let their guard down and overshare.

YouTubers may perceive the insulation of an "online" world gives them additional protection from oversharing. This is a gross misunderstanding of the internet and context in general. While an anonymous account provides protection from oversharing, a public figure cannot rely on separation of location for protection. For example, a politician doesn't rely on the protection of keeping their "personal account" and "official office account" on social media separately. Anything they say in any forum or context will inevitably find its way into a different context because there is no firewall protecting the flow of information.

All of the oversharing of information, and those insecurities and anxieties of that information, are weaponized by trolls against the lolcow. In fact, lots of the information used by trolls was not uncovered with investigative journalism but offered up to the trolls by the creator themself. There is a reason why the police tell you, "Anything you say or do can be used against you."

Trait #7: Personality Flaws

Of all the traits, this might be the most important. It should be made very clear that personality flaws are different from mental illness or mental handicaps. Mental handicap, or developmental disability, are various chronic conditions which limit communication, social interaction, mobility, or overall functionality. Mental illness is a clinical disorder which controls thoughts, emotions, or behaviors which is recognized by the medical community. Personality flaws are matters of behavior or character that can be pathological.

All lolcows have some personality flaw: greed, entitlement, narcissism, enlarged ego, delusions of grandeur, etc. The compounding effect of these personality flaws, in combination with other factors, is inability to change.

How do we know that personality flaws affect someone into becoming a lolcow? Because these personality flaws translate into difficulties in the personal lives of the lolcow as well as the online world. From the lolcow's perspective, they don't have this successful and vibrant life outside of the internet. The difficulties they have online are the same difficulties they have in real life: isolation, ridicule, failure, etc.

These personality flaws create isolation. These flaws isolate them from their friends and family in the real world. In the online world, these flaws isolate them from fellow YouTubers. Any real human relationship must have a give-and-take element. This is universally understood. The creator's collaboration partners, or co-workers, are usually pushed away and become increasingly frustrated by a one-sided friendship.

Trait #8: Unable to Build a New Audience or Reinvent Themselves

Despite the common sense need for structural reform of their YouTube channel and content, lolcows remain obstinate and continue their course. This is related to Trait #2 - Bad Content and Trait #7 - Personality Flaws.

There is a deadly combination of being creatively bankrupt combined with laziness and no self-awareness. It makes it impossible to progress a career in content creation.

Trait #9: Financially Desperate

Because lolcows refuse to get jobs and their content is not very monetizable, they have very little income. This shouldn't be a problem in many cases. Many YouTubers, at the growth, peak, and even into the stagnation phase, still have high incomes. A reasonable and common-sense approach would be to save and invest money. This nest egg would provide for any shortfall in income. However, lolcows suffer from financial mismanagement. This is usually driven by Trait #7 - Personality Flaws and Trait #3 - Menial Job. Personality flaws cloud the lolcow's judgement, and many do not plan ahead for possible down years. Having a menial job prior means they did not obtain high income previously or gain financial literacy. These things in combination mean they are unable to effectively and reasonably handle money.

To be fair, it is not uncommon for people who gain financial success very quickly to lose their money. There are countless professional athletes, actors, and musicians who made tens of millions of dollars over the course of their career and still end up bankrupt. Even people who win the lottery go bankrupt. Wasteful spending and a false belief the money train will continue leave many creators with barely enough to scrape by later in their career.

Trait #10: Inability to Quit Being a Public Figure

A lolcow finds it very hard to disengage from the online world. Most good-faith observers would look at their situation and diagnose that drastic reforms are needed to save their YouTube career or would recommend moving on to something else. Lolcows seem unable to make either choice. They remain public figures for personal and financial reasons.

They are unable to quit because of Trait #7 - Personality Flaws. Usually, this is related to their narcissism and ego. They require the public limelight to feed these pathological tendencies. This is also related to Trait #1 - Parasocial Relationship with the Audience. Most lolcows do not have friends offline either. They incorrectly use the internet as a friend, crutch, or surrogate to stave off their depressing loneliness. This deadly combination of narcissism and the need for companionship keeps the lolcow online and engaged. It keeps them engaged with fans, which can be useful in the growth and peak states of their career, but it also compels them to engage with trolls.

There are also financial incentives that keep them online. We will discuss this in a future chapter regarding the *Lolcow Gap.*

Chapter 5: The Lolcow Biography

We will review the story of six distinct lolcows in the following chapters. While hearing their story, you can start to see the pattern emerge - the traits of the lolcow become increasingly clear.

Why did I pick these lolcows? I wanted to pick a diverse group across different eras and genres of content. These biographies are just the tip of the iceberg when it comes to the lolcows. The "lore" associated with our cast of characters runs deep. What I have presented is an abbreviated version.

Successful creators are successful because of their production or their persona. There are some people who are all production, some have persona and production, and some are all persona. Your public persona is a "front" that you put on, but it's not outright dishonesty. It's part of being an entertainer and public figure. It also sets you apart from everyone else. Your persona isn't totally fake. It's based on reality but is a pseudo reconstruction of yourself.

There are people whose end product is so important that it doesn't really matter what their persona is. For example, Roman Polanski was a talented filmmaker. Despite being a convicted child rapist, he got a standing ovation at the Oscars and 160 directors, actors, screenwriters, and producers signed a petition for his release when he was jailed. This principle also extends to other non-entertainment fields. In sports, think of players who have controversies that come up. If they're a star player and very talented, the team is more than willing to overlook "indiscretions". But as soon as that player's in-game performance suffers, they are dropped like a benchwarmer. In the science field, the same principle applies. Wernher Von

Braun was a Nazi scientist that developed the V-2 Rocket (using slave labor) that killed tens of thousands of people. However, his knowledge of rocketry and advanced technology was too valuable. After WW2, he was hired by NASA. Both the United States and the Soviet Union made use of former Nazi scientists in the space race.

Some people have production and persona. For example, Walt Disney, a pioneer in animation. Everyone has watched a Disney movie, I don't have to explain his production. He also had a persona. It was one of the most carefully crafted and successful personas. He was "Uncle Walt". His Uncle Walt persona was a warm, wholesome, fatherly figure for his company and employees. In reality, he was a perfectionist, sometimes a control freak, an ambitious captain of industry, and chain smoker. Now, it's not fair to say his positive qualities were all fake. Most people who knew Walt Disney liked him. But his Uncle Walt persona was the best side of himself.

Walt Disney was acutely aware of this persona. As we discussed in the prior chapter, Disney had the prudence of a public figure. He existed in the studio system of checks and balances, since he worked in the collaborative field of movie production. Even as the head of the company, he could be kept in check by his trusted brother (and often unsung hero), Roy Disney. He also predated the internet, so it was a lot easier to control information back then.

There are public figures based around persona. Liberace was a piano player known for everything except for being a piano player. He was known as "Mr. Showmanship". He was one of the highest paid performers of the 1950s and early 1960s. His presentation was everything. He wore elaborate costumes, made grand entrances on stage, and basically trademarked the candelabra on the piano. His persona was magnetic. He was warm, interactive, approachable, family oriented, devoutly Christian, and fun. He added "schmaltz" and pageantry to his performances. He was a television pioneer - he spoke directly to the camera like an old friend or neighbor. His carefully crafted persona concealed his homosexuality, which would have destroyed anybody's career back in the 1950s.

Liberace was one of the most famous piano players of his era. But nobody remembers him for his piano playing ability. That's not to say he was a bad player or couldn't play. Liberace was a decent piano player, but not good enough to be a traditional concert pianist. Music critics often derided his playing. But he simply shrugged it off stating, "...I laughed all the way to the bank." (Foster) And he was financially very successful and adored by a mainly female audience.

Failure to maintain a creator's persona results in the audience leaving. When Liberace was engaged, he received so much negative fan mail from his female fans that he broke off the engagement to maintain his persona as an eligible bachelor.

Let's look at another example where there are many creators with a nearly identical product where persona is everything. Every traditional channel has a late-night comedian/late-night show. Their content and formula are nearly identical. Why would someone watch Stephen Colbert over Jimmy Kimmel? Or watch Jimmy Fallon over Seth Meyers? The "content" of the show is very similar; the only difference is the persona. Who do you like better?

Being a YouTuber doesn't usually involve a lot of production. They rely on persona. "Broadcast Yourself" remember? Particularly in the earlier days of YouTube, the production value was very low. There is also a much larger range of competitors. Using late night TV as an example, there are only a few TV channels. On YouTube, in any particular genre, there are thousands or tens of thousands of competitors.

The competition is higher now than it ever was. Most YouTubers can't compete on production. Most lack the resources and skills to compete with even basic television shows. Therefore, they have to compete on persona. Because they make content outside of the studio system, they have more creative freedom with constructing their persona. Their persona is their most valuable asset. The destruction of this delicate persona would destroy their career. In any other media, it would be carefully controlled and moderated by their agent or manager.

However, as we will read in the following chapters. All lolcows eventually have their original persona destroyed. Usually, this is self-inflicted. Their persona is destroyed by oversharing information (Trait #6) and their personality flaws (Trait #7) becoming increasingly visible.

Many YouTubers, and these lolcows, were noteworthy because of their persona. Once this persona was shattered, they couldn't stand out from the thousands of other creators. They then slip into obscurity outside of a regular audience. As part of their fall from grace, they attract another audience. This is the very niche detractor audience. These detractors enjoy hate-watching their content.

Chapter 6: DarkSydePhil aka Philip Burnell

Philip Burnell has had a very long career as an online content creator. He is most known by his moniker: DSP or DarkSydePhil. He has called himself the "King of Hate". He is also known as the "internet cockroach" due to his unlikability, but also as a reference to his ever-present existence on the internet and seemingly unkillable career.

The Wild West was a period of American history that we all know from Westerns. There were huge expanses of wilderness. Pioneers and settlers moved from the East into the new frontier driven by ideas of Manifest Destiny. Miners wanted to strike it rich prospecting gold. Farmers wanted to settle down on their own land or work as a cowboy. Many went to work building the railroad.

How did the Wild West die? Barbed wire, a simple invention. No longer did you need cowboys. We built the railroad and expanded infrastructure. This led to the growth of towns and cities which brought law enforcement and an end to lawlessness. And people brought their families, eventually evening out the population distribution across the country. By 1890, the Census Bureau declared the frontier had closed, as there was no longer a discernable line between settlement and significant areas of uninhabited land.

There was no infrastructure for video sharing online before YouTube. You had to have your own website. YouTube was like the railroad for independent video content creation on the internet. Millions of creators flocked to the site and created their own channels. Just like people used to build towns from scratch in the Wild West. Some of these towns were boom towns turned into ghost towns and are now gone. Others carry on still as small towns. And some towns grow into big towns. And those big towns grow into cities. People like Philip Burnell were those early pioneers and channels like DSPGaming were those towns.

Burnell has been called one of the early pioneers of the video game genre on YouTube. His story is the story of the early days on the site. This YouTube doesn't exist anymore. Technology moves so fast that in a young person's lifetime, the entire website can change. The YouTube ecosystem in 2007 was like Los Angeles in 1880, when it was a city of only 12,000 people. The Los Angeles Valley was one of farmers and ranchers. And in one person's lifetime, it was transformed into a city of 2 million people. In 10 years, YouTube's Wild West era was over; he website had totally transformed.

Burnell's channel is not Los Angeles, CA, but is more akin to Tombstone, AZ. A very early town which has the same population it did in 1890. Burnell exists as a living fossil or an internet curiosity. He didn't so much build a career online, but it fell into his lap. Like a Wild West prospector drinking out of a stream and finding a gold nugget. In an interview with TheQuartering, in September of 2019, he said "I never planned on doing this to make any money, like it just fell in my lap out of nowhere overnight. I was like, oh crap this is amazing. I'm making more money now than I ever did at my office job. For 5 years I was working there, and they laid me off. And I'm making, like, so much more money. It's crazy." (TheQuartering, 2019) His failure to maintain or manage his accidental success doomed his career.

Philip Burnell was born in April of 1982 in Connecticut. Before he was an online creator, he worked for a helicopter company. He worked in the office, not as a pilot or mechanic. Throughout the mid to late 2000s, he was active in the *Street Fighter* video game scene. *Street Fighter* is a popular fighting arcade game going back to the 1990s. He competed in in-person tournaments up and down the East Coast. Burnell was known for his combative attitude at best, which was rude and disruptive at worst. He didn't shy away from that criticism and embraced it. He became known as the "King of Hate".

Success

Burnell has been a lolcow for so long, you have to go back to the early days of YouTube when he was considered successful. How did Burnell achieve success on YouTube in the first place? Burnell became successful by pointing a camera at the television and recording himself playing video games with commentary over it. He also reviewed fast food. Burnell had first mover advantage in the Let's Play genre on YouTube.

He began uploading YouTube videos in the late 2000s. At this time, there was very little monetization on the platform. Video game content was not monetizable because of the enforcement of copyright laws at the time. Video game makers could flag a video for copyright infringement and frequently did.

Copyright laws are always shifting and evolving as new technology emerges. For example, when Betamax and VHS were introduced in the 1980s, TV and film studios wanted to make home recordings of television copyright infringement. The Supreme Court in *Sony Corp. of America v. Universal City Studios, Inc. (1984)*, ruled that *time shifting*, recording TV so you can play it back later, was fair use. And instead of destroying the TV and film industry, home recordings enhanced profitability. People bought home movies, rented home videos, and consumed more content thanks to home video.

The same happened with video game Let's Plays or various other video game content. Let's Plays are a style of YouTube content where a video game playthrough is overland with commentary. In the early days of YouTube, pre-2007, there was no monetization. In 2007, YouTube launched the Partner Program where you could get monetized. By 2010, there were multi-channel networks like Machinima (which Burnell joined) that allowed a YouTuber to be protected from copyright claims as they would have this larger media company backing them.

Let's Plays exploded in popularity in the early 2010s and video game publishers began issuing copyright strikes. Particularly aggressive were Japanese companies like Nintendo and Sega, as Japan has strict copyright laws. Nintendo went so far as to create their own Nintendo Creators Program so they could try to get revenue from Let's Plays.

Why did the video game companies care if people were making Let's Plays? It was the same reasoning why TV and film studios were against Betamax/VHS recording; they thought it would take away from profits. Instead of people buying video games, people would just watch other people play video games. However, by 2014 it was widely accepted Let's Plays increased profits and acted as free advertising. And it makes sense. If you see people having fun playing the game, that makes you want to buy the game and play it too. By 2015, Let's Plays were widely accepted as fair use.

Burnell's success came from being one of the very first Let's Play channels. He did consistent uploads across several different game genres. There was very little competition for him in the pre-2010 era because it wasn't monetizable. When he was laid off from his job in 2010, he decided to focus full time on YouTube. He had already been uploading regularly on YouTube under his original channel

DarkSydePhil from 2008 to 2010. He started his next channel, DSP Gaming, in April of 2010. He also made game reviews in his *The Hateful Truth* series and non-game reviews in his *DSP Tries It* series.

When Burnell signed with Machinima in 2010 and was able to monetize his content, he had a first mover advantage over any other creator trying to do Let's Plays because his channel and audience were already built up. By 2012, Burnell was at his peak. But even in 2012, he was lagging behind the times. He didn't want to do edited content. He was still recording videos with a camera in front of a television. That may have cut it in 2008, but by this point capture cards (recording directly from the TV) were the base level of production value viewers expected.

The other issue Burnell ran into was that he wasn't very good at playing video games. Detractor and troll channels ran series like: *This is how you DON'T Play,* and others where they highlighted Burnell struggling to make his way through games. He frequently got frustrated or angry. He then blamed the video game for his failures. When he played online, he would blame cheating or lag when he lost.

The *Streisand Effect* is a phenomenon where someone's attempt to censor or hide information backfires, resulting in it gaining more public attention. It is named after singer Barbara Streisand, who filed a lawsuit against a photographer for publishing a photo of her mansion online. Streisand's lawsuit brought massive attention to the photo, which had only been viewed on the photographer's website six times before her lawsuit. Because the lawsuit gained media attention, the website was visited over 400,000 times - having the opposite effect of what the lawsuit was supposed to do. (Davis, 2025)

By 2013, Burnell was losing viewership. He continued to battle the detractors against him. He issued copyright strikes against channels making fun of his bad gameplay. These troll/detractor channels, which were tiny compared to his channel, experienced massive growth because of the Streisand Effect. More and more detractors started making videos of Burnell and going through his enormous back catalogue of videos to mock him.

In 2015, he had "The Incident". Burnell streamed himself masturbating. He did not realize the camera was still on. The video was not graphic, as it only showed him chest up. But it was a very embarrassing moment and became instant troll fodder.

Lolcow Status

This should have been the end of Burnell's story. He was one of the very first creators to have a large channel of monetized video game content on YouTube. His dedication to his hobby, i.e. his consistent upload schedule and volume of videos put him in the right place, at the right time, once monetization became possible. By 2013, he was already supplanted by funnier, more entertaining, and better gamers. They had better production value. His fuddy-duddy gameplay was out of style. By 2015, his mainstream unironic career was over.

So, why are we talking about this guy 10 years after his career ended? Burnell is known as the "internet cockroach" for a reason. What Burnell is most known for is not his early days; it's being a lolcow. The basis for the dislike for Burnell is mainly around his humorous volatile reactions and dislikeable personality.

I spoke with a detractor channel, *Gamer Face Gaming*. He posts humorous photos of Burnell's face while gaming. It could be Burnell looking miserable, confused, or bored. He stated, "Ever watch those 'reality shows'? DSP is like one of those but not by choice." He continued later stating, "So, why watch DSP if he is that bad? I think some watch just to follow up on whats going to happen next. He got a girlfriend. He got kicked out of Machinima? He got a bankruptcy? He got married? Once you get introduced into the 'vortex' you kind of follow him just to watch whats going to happen next."

The largest complaint about Burnell is his incessant e-begging. He will *constantly* ask for financial support. It is so egregious there are detractors who keep a running tally of how many times he asks for money in a single stream or day. He can ask for money as much as 80 to well over 100 times a stream.

Burnell uses what could be considered manipulation to get money from viewers. He "rewards" his audience once they reach the "goal". This goal is an arbitrary dollar amount set by Burnell. These "rewards" the audience gets are meaningless. For example, the audience gets to watch him eat fast food. On a good day, the audience might even get to *pick* the fast food he eats and then they can enjoy watching him eat the fast food on stream. (Usually, he doesn't let the audience pick the fast food.) He might also put on a special hat. Or Burnell might put on a vest. He has also been criticized for changing the goals. For example, he stated for $100 he will put on a vest. And then once reaching that goal, "rug pulls" the viewers and increases the goal to $150.

Burnell reacts to everything in an abnormal way. For example, when he struggles to open packaging for food or other items he vents his frustration at the people working at the factory. When struggling to open a bottle of water, he remarked that the people at the factory "filled it too much".

While playing video games, he reacts very poorly to setbacks and dying in game. Getting frustrated while playing games is normal. It happens to everyone. Burnell takes it to a whole new level. He will blame lag, other players cheating, the game mechanics, glitches, his internet provider, worn out game controller, or any excuse that he can think of - except for his lack of gaming skill or someone else playing the game better than him.

Burnell will use his frustration as an opportunity to ask for money. BroSydePhil, a detractor channel, stated, "I think I could deal with the rage, the whole 'this sucks', what I have a hard time with is when he says things like, 'this is f**king bulls**t' then he looks over and says, '*Now guys*, here I am suffering through this game, having a bad time, and I'm not getting anything for it'. Oh my god. How are you real!?" (That Being Said, 2025)

Another layer of dislike, or disgust, Burnell's detractors have for him is the "grifts" he pulls off are against his audience of mainly autistic and special needs viewers. Agent Proper, a detractor channel against DSP, told me, "I would describe Phil as a narcissistic middle-aged man, who takes advantage of his audience of sad lonely individuals who are majority of the time are handicapped in some way [mentally/physically]. Phil tries to play the victim at any opportunity while trying to be the hero at the same time."

In 1956, sociologists Donald Horton and R. Richard Wohl described the phenomenon in their article *Mass Communication and Para-Social Interaction*. They were studying radio, television, and movies and the "illusion" of face-to-face relationships. Later in the article, they describe "Extreme Para-Sociability":

"For the great majority of the audience, the para-social is complementary to normal social life. It provides a social milieu in which the everyday assumptions and understandings of primary group interaction and sociability are demonstrated and reaffirmed. The 'personality' program, however, is peculiarly favorable to the formation of compensatory attachments <u>by the socially isolated, the socially inept, the aged and invalid, the timid and rejected.</u> The persona himself is readily available as an object of love – especially when he succeeds in cultivating the recommended quality of 'heart.' Nothing could be more reasonable or natural than that people who are isolated and lonely should seek sociability and love wherever they think they can find it. It is only when the para-social relationship becomes a substitute for autonomous social participation, when it proceeds in absolute defiance of objective reality, that it can be regarded as pathological." (Horton & Wohl, 1956, 226)

According to trolls/detractors, the unironic viewers of Burnell who financially support him are mentally handicapped. It's been theorized why Burnell's content appeals to people with autism. He has a very strict schedule, very consistently uploads videos, is constantly present, and frequently overexplains things, sometimes in circles. For example, he will explain for 20 to 40 minutes at a time: his daily schedule, what a department store is, the weather outside, or other minutiae about his life. Also, lacking social awareness themselves, they don't seem to be bothered by Burnell's constant e-begging.

Trolls have tracked down many viewers who have donated to Burnell. In interviews, many of these unironic viewers said they looked up to Burnell. Some saw him as an older father figure to them. Or they appreciated his constant online presence. Many had been fans going back to his early days online. Many of these fans, who have very limited financial means themselves, admitted to giving Burnell thousands of dollars over the years. (And yes, because Burnell has so few authentic fans, it is possible you can track many of them down.) Let's not be too hard on these people. Burnell's constant e-begging is very similar to megachurch preachers or other grifters. They prey on sad, compromised, or desperate people.

Ashton Parks aka PPP of the web show *Kino Casino* remarked, "Phil really is, just to any sort of outside observer or anything, just so f**king boring. Just a black hole of content. Total 'non-tent'. Total charisma vacuum. But if you are in his orbit, if you are watching his streams for long enough, you will discover why people hate him. You will discover why he really is a total f**king piece of s**t. Like, once I actually started paying attention to him, it was just like, *woah buddy*!" (Kino Casino Clips, 2025). If you want to know why Burnell is disliked, you can tune into one of his streams and see for yourself.

Burnell's interesting lolcow moments happen in "arcs". These arcs are a departure from the normal grind of Burnell's never-ending war against the trolls/detractors and daily uploads of "non-tent". We will cover 3 arcs in the remainder of his chapter: the bankruptcy arc, *Side Scrollers* arc, and the King Snake arc.

Bankruptcy & Bank Leak Arc

Burnell's dire financial position became featured more in his streams as he faded with relevancy after 2015. He had strict "goals" for his streams and will continually ask for money and donations (e-begging) to make it to the goals. His pleas of financial dire straits and insecurity became cannon fodder for trolls. It was debated if Burnell was pleading poverty as a guilt trip or he really was in trouble.

In January of 2020, Burnell filed for Chapter 7 bankruptcy. It was a boomtime for trolls and detractors. Because bankruptcy filings are public records, there was finally a window into Burnell's private life to confirm all the detractors' and trolls' suspicions. Also, to expose Burnell's lies. It turns out that while Burnell's audience was fading, his income was still strong. Burnell was making $8,000 to $10,000 a month in the six months prior to his bankruptcy filing. (Smith, 2020)

Because it was a virtual hearing due to Covid-19, the trolls attended the bankruptcy hearings. They also began poring over the documents. Burnell had excessive consumer credit card debt. His liabilities totaled over $131,000, and this included $15,000 in back taxes to the IRS. Many criticized Burnell for lying in bankruptcy documents and misrepresenting facts. For example, Burnell claimed he had over $5,000 a month in operating expenses as a video game streamer. (Smith, 2020)

This disclosure of finances also seemingly confirmed Burnell's addiction to *WWE Champions*. What is *WWE Champions*? It's a mobile game similar to *Candy Crush*. Because Burnell's account on *WWE Champions* is so high up on the leaderboards, the only way you can get that high is using the "pay to win" elements of the game. These totaled tens of thousands of dollars per year. Burnell denied for years he was spending excessively on *WWE Champions*. He publicly stated he stopped playing mobile games in 2018. He also went back and forth on whether he played it or not. His constant denial and battling with the trolls/detractors over this issue went on for years.

Burnell had to list his business expenses as part of his bankruptcy. But these expenses were not itemized. It's not clear how Burnell could spend $3,000 to $9,000 a month on the "business" of being a video game streamer. There is no overhead. The only thing he could be spending money on is utilities and buying video games. However, he claimed he only had $1,500 in business assets. (Smith, 2020) It was speculated Burnell was hiding his *WWE Champions* addiction in his business expenses. Because he was a video game streamer and *WWE Champions* is a video game (despite never playing the game on stream), the government was ignorant of the discrepancy. Because this was a personal bankruptcy, Burnell's business expenses were not scrutinized by his creditors or the court.

The trolls and detractors were annoyed Burnell was able to get through bankruptcy court without his lies being revealed. But they went to work and began to catalogue Phil's earnings.

A troll was able to determine through calling Bank of America and reverse engineering Burnell's social security number, they were able to recall the last 10 transactions. Through continuously calling, the troll was able to create a spreadsheet of 500 transactions cataloguing Burnell's spending for 18 months. This spreadsheet was then posted on the internet forum site, KiwiFarms.

People began poring through the bank leaks. By reverse engineering the spending amounts and destination of the payments, the trolls assert Burnell spent $44,950.30 on video game microtransactions. (Smith, 2020) Most likely *WWE Champions*. That was 25% of his household spending. Burnell wasn't able to get the police involved because it would confirm that it was his bank account. Burnell tried to deny the leaks. But he also uses them to bait sympathy from the audience by claiming persecution by the trolls.

Side Scrollers Arc

Side Scrollers is a podcast run by Craig Skistimas aka Stuttering Craig and Adam Cringler. They mainly discuss video game topics. Burnell allowed himself to be interviewed by them on March 16, 2023. Burnell does not give many interviews. Because the "lore" surrounding Burnell is so long and he is culturally irrelevant, many people don't have all the information about him. If you were to cover every arc and every controversy with Burnell, it would be over 100 pages.

Craig and Cringler were not completely familiar with Burnell's history. Many trolls and detractors messaged them ahead of time trying to provide them information. However, their open book approach worked in their favor as Burnell dug himself into a hole throughout the entire five hour long interview. Even though they were not armed with many of the facts the regular Burnell troll/detractor would be privy to, just using common sense they were able to poke holes in his story. Burnell wasn't able to blow them off, and they pressed him on many details.

They confronted Burnell about some of his edgy racial humor he said in the past. (Side Scrollers, 2023) They confronted Burnell about his $5,000 per month business expenses. Burnell feigned ignorance and said he didn't know what his business expenses were. They pressed him about the bank leaks. Burnell said it was not him.

And finally, they pressed him on his addiction to *WWE Champions*. Burnell admitted to playing *WWE Champions*, but not as the account linked to him previously. Craig quickly proposed a way to disprove the trolls. Burnell could privately send Craig (as an independent third party) a screenshot of his *WWE Champions* account , which Burnell declined. Then his "internet went out" and disconnected. When Burnell came back to the podcast, which would have given him time to manufacture another account, Craig rescinded his offer to vouch for Burnell.

The troll and detractor community erupted as someone was finally able to confront Burnell. Burnell's five-hour long interview was mainly him digging his own grave. Refusing even a simple test was treated by the internet as confirmation of his *WWE Champions* addiction. Burnell would later go on to attack Craig and Cringler, and *Side Scrollers* in various ways.

King Snake Arc

Kino Casino is a web show hosted by Andy Warski and Ashton Parks aka PPP. It's a comedy show which covers internet drama. Their show is part troll, part detractor, and part journalist. What follows is a complicated web of back and forth between them and Burnell.

Burnell began collaborating with *Kino Casino* in August of 2024. He would appear on their show. Seeing Burnell collaborate with anyone was rare. For Burnell's audience, it was unclear why Burnell would work with *Kino Casino*, who are well-known for internet drama. And for the *Kino Casino* audience it was strange why they would platform Burnell, a known lolcow.

As Warski and PPP would later describe on *Kino Casino*, they were purposely ingratiating themselves with Burnell. They would "glaze him" and sing his praises. This would lead to many personal conversations with both hosts. These personal conversations would then lead to additional troll fodder that they would bring up at a later point.

Burnell was mainly ignorant of this fact and despite warnings from his fans that *Kino Casino* would "snake" him, he continued to defend them publicly. To "snake someone" is internet parlance to betray someone.

On March 14, 2025, *Kino Casino* broke ties with Burnell and uploaded a section of the livestream to their YouTube channel titled: "DARK SYDE PHIL GETS SNAKED! ALL BRIDGES BURNT!" (Kino Casino Clips, 2025) In this two hour video, they revealed many embarrassing details about Burnell. Burnell wanted to see Warski's abs. Burnell called Warski his "gaming soul mate", which they found cringeworthy and awkward. They were bombarded with messages and comments from Burnell, which they found as him being desperate for attention and validation. They described his life as a sad shut-in and hermit. They also mock him for being a closeted homosexual. They found him difficult or even impossible to work with. Burnell would lecture them and express his frustration when they would direct message him on his "day off", but then message and demand they respond to him on their days off. They described Burnell as selfish and one-sided. For example, asking them not to stream in "his" time slot, even though their audience was 10 times larger.

On March 25, 2025, Burnell posted a five hour long live stream titled "The FULL Kino Casino Snaking Saga ENDS!". (DSPGaming, 2025) Burnell then leaked their private messages. *Kino Casino* then leaked other messages. Burnell would later claim that he was "the king snake" and he was always secretly going to betray *Kino Casino*. He thought of himself as the "king snake". A king snake is an apex predator that eats other snakes.

This set off the fabled *infinite money glitch* of content for *Kino Casino*. The infinite money glitch is internet slang for a loophole or system you can exploit to generate endless money. They would cover Burnell and then Burnell would respond. They would then react to Burnell's response and mock him. Burnell would defend himself. They would then make content off his response. This cycle continues to this day.

On October 3, 2025, *Kino Casino* released *The Dented Zone*. It is a parody movie about Burnell's life in the style of the television show, *The Twilight Zone*. Warski played Burnell and PPP played Burnell's wife and other characters. They mocked Burnell for being a closeted homosexual, his sexless marriage, his overweight wife, Burnell's long winded repetitive rants, alcoholism, neuroticism, and most of all, his repetitive sad existence. The video stands at over 130,000 views as of writing. (Kino Casino Clips, 2025)

Burnell repeatedly responded to *Kino Casino*. They continue to respond back to mock and "felt" him (to use their parlance).

The Sad Life

Burnell's relevancy is based on his continual, never ending, and futile fight against the trolls and detractors. Burnell still streams to 150-500 people daily. There is a dedicated cottage industry of troll and detractor channels that make content around him and use his reactions to make more content off him. Their content mocks and ridicules him for his e-begging, lies, crash outs, and rants.

Philip Burnell did not respond to a request for comment.

Troll names:
DarkSydeBeg
Master of All Games
The Blamer

Other memes:

Snort fort - a term used for Burnell's home. "Snort" references Burnell's tendency to snort between sentences and "fort" being his house.

Dents - the pejorative term the trolls/detractors use for Burnell's unironic viewers, "pay pigs", or "whales"; because their brains are "dented".

Auditing the dents - Burnell's lectures about the lack of support or monetary contributions. He guilt trips the audience into sending money.

Pignosis - Burnell's "spell" that he puts on his *paypigs* (another word for whales) to keep them entranced and giving him money.

Snort Korea – a troll term for Burnell's channel. A play on "North Korea" and "snort". It refers to his excessive use of banning and censoring his chat.

You can use this QR Code to access Burnell's main YouTube channel:

Chapter 7: WingsofRedemption aka Jordie Jordan

Jordie Jordan was born in Conway, South Carolina in 1986 and grew up in a rural working-class household. He has spoken about his difficulties with health and excessive weight from a young age. Limited financial means and an introverted personality contributed to his early reliance on video games for entertainment and social connection.

He was working a factory job when he launched his YouTube channel, WingsofRedemption, in 2009. His earliest content focused on gameplay commentary, primarily within the *Call of Duty* franchise making Call of Duty Commentary. Call of Duty Commentary is exactly what it sounds like. People put commentary over their gameplay of *Call of Duty*. At this time, YouTube's gaming scene was still in its formative years. Jordan's commentary came with an analytical approach to multiplayer strategy which allowed him to build a following.

In 2010, Jordan became a co-founder of the *Painkiller Already* (PKA) podcast, alongside Woody'sGamertag (Matthew Woodworth) and FPSRussia (Kyle Myers). The podcast combined gaming topics with off-topic discussion, interviews, and humor. *PKA* significantly expanded Jordan's visibility within the gaming community.

Jordan's contributions to *PKA* were many humorous stories from his life. These later became troll fodder. He told a story about having to put down a dog, but instead of going to a veterinarian, he took the dog out to the swamp and shot it. His family had a dog named "n*****r" growing up. He thought you needed a passport to cross state lines. He also told a story about being so constipated he had to be administered a saline enema by his grandmother. Then, "the turd went sideways on me". He fell off the toilet and hit his head, requiring the assistance of his grandmother to remove the fecal matter that was stuck in his rectum. (PKA Clips, 2024) These stories were told in good fun and, at least at this stage, Jordan seemed okay with socializing and sometimes being the butt of the joke. (no pun intended)

Cracks Beginning to Form

The first signs of trouble for Jordan's career were beginning to show during his time on *PKA*. During a *PKA* show, a guest, Syndicate aka Thomas Cassell, verbally sparred with Jordan regarding their gaming skill. This led to a 1v1 match in *Call of Duty*. *Call of Duty* was Jordan's specialty. Jordan ultimately lost the match and exploded with anger. He "rage quit" the game and insulted Syndicate. His inability to be a good sport in defeat garnered him much negative attention. (Knudsen, 2019)

Jordan collaborated with FPSRussia aka Kyle Myers, by staying in his house for a time and filming weight loss training videos. This "bootcamp" was seen as good content at the time. However, living with Kyle highlighted his lack of social graces. Jordan's own insecurity about his weight was also featured in the content. Eventually, he gave up on the bootcamp and returned home.

Jordan's tenure on *PKA* continued to be contentious. He clashed with co-hosts, reacted defensively to jokes at his expense, and expressed frustration with the show's dynamic. These conflicts, along with his growing sensitivity to online criticism, ultimately led to his diminished role.

The final straw was a survivalist trip in the woods which was planned between the hosts. Jordan agreed to go. While Kyle and Woody were on their way, Jordan decided not to rendezvous with the group, but he did not tell anyone. This lack of common courtesy and disregard for his fellow hosts led to them to booting him off the show. This left him isolated online.

Open Season for Trolling

By the mid-2010s, Jordan's focus shifted from YouTube uploads, which were edited and prerecorded, to livestreaming on Twitch. Jordan's streams frequently included candid discussions about his personal life, finances, and health. This provided trolls with material to exploit. Streaming also allowed for real-time interaction with viewers and exposed Jordan to constant trolling. This trolling included "stream sniping", sabotaging his online games, and sending heckling and demeaning super chats. This trolling also escalated to swatting and hacking his online gaming accounts. Jordan's constant reactions to this trolling ranged from angry, where he would yell and throw controllers, to desperate pleading, including breaking down in tears. This trolling and reaction to trolling became defining features of his broadcasts. (Knudsen, 2019)

This vicious cycle of trolling and his reaction to trolling eventually became a cottage industry. Entire YouTube channels were dedicating themselves to documenting his behavior, creating "highlight" compilations of his outbursts, and mocking his personal struggles. These troll channels included: Sean Ranklin, Wing Tings, Lord of the Wings, GulagKingpin, BreakingBanquet, Lummox: A Hired Hoodlum, Wings 007, and others. Other channels, like Liquid Richard, created four full albums of music using remixed voice clips of Jordan and referencing other memes of the troll community. While some of these channels are no longer active, there is always some new account being created to satisfy the demand for WingsofRedemption detractor/troll content.

For example, in an infamous video uploaded by Sean Ranklin in 2018 titled, "wingsofredemption gets stream sniped and loses it". (Ranklin, 2019) it showed Jordan playing *Call of Duty*. He repeatedly gets killed over and over again, getting more and more angry as the match progresses. A teammate in the game repeatedly blocks him from shooting enemies by standing in front of him - a classic troll tactic. Jordan asks the viewers, "If somebody could please like get me their [the troll's] information …like their name, their address, their number, how I can get in contact with these guys I would really like to know because like I'm seriously considering suing them. Because at this point, they're going to follow me around when I stream and they're affecting my business at this point. Honestly, they're affecting my, they're affecting my ability to make money."

Jordan gets more and more upset as he reads the livestream's chat. Eventually he gets so mad he throws his controller down on the desk and yells, "Look here! Look listen! Appearing offline does not f**king stop it! So stop giving f**king advice you know nothing about!" And later states, "I'm banning anyone trying to give me advice. Real talk."

Later in the stream, Jordan gets killed again in *Call of Duty* again. In his frustration, he throws his controller across the room. He then gets up from the desk and goes to the back wall of his room. He faces the wall silently, then yells, "F**k!" and punches the wall. He then proceeds to somberly walk back to his chair and sit down.

While at his desk, Jordan has an emotional breakdown. "I give up. I don't know when I'll stream again." As he bursts into tears he exclaims, "I really need to make this f**king money. I really wanted to get this f**king [weight loss] surgery man. I wanted it so f**king bad." He throws his controller against the desk again while shouting, "I can't do it. I can't take this s**t no more man!" He continues to cry and says, "All I wanted to do was like, I was f**king lonely, I wanted to f**king stream and have a good time. Have a good game." He then breaks down in tears and says, "I hate my life." (Ranklin, 2019)

These emotional outbursts, reacting to trolling, and annoyance at streaming would continue to be fixtures of Jordan's streams. I reached out to Sean Ranklin, one of the most prominent troll channels of that era. Ranklin advised me, "He would consistently have these 'disaster streams' where he made a complete embarrassment of himself and delete the streams, pretending like they never happened. He would ignore any and all advice on how to improve himself. This is IMO one of the biggest things he gets criticized for. People try to help him, he ignores it, then people stop trying to help and just watch for content. Kyle and Woody TRIED SO MANY TIMES on PKA to motivate and inspire him."

Nothing Changes

Jordan eventually did get the weight loss surgery in June of 2018. As he went back to streaming, he lamented his life didn't really change. His failure to lose weight became another point of trolling. He was trolled as having "beat the surgery". The surgery is supposed to have a high success rate for helping people to lose weight, but he continued to appear around 400 pounds.

Jordan began taking anti-depressants around this time and his emotional outbursts started to diminish. Trolls could still get to him to react by sending troll donations. The donation, along with a written message shown on screen, and sometimes Jordan would read them aloud. Because these donations were a steady source of income for him, he continued to read them, and the trolls continued to get a reaction.

Throughout 2020, Jordan became embroiled in another controversy. In October of 2020, his grandmother, who he lived with and took care of him most of his life, died of cancer. Instead of going to her funeral, he decided to stream video games, drawing lots of criticism online. Jordan also got married in 2020 to a woman called Kelly who would appear in his content.

Jordan had his Twitch partnership status terminated on July 26, 2021. Jordan was banned from Twitch for violation of content guidelines. It was suspected that trolls reported his channel.

Jordan began driving for DoorDash sometime in 2021 for supplemental income. Instead of keeping this information to himself, he began discussing it on his stream. It quickly got the attention of trolls. He was banned from DoorDash on October 9, 2021 as he announced this on Twitter. (Hale, 2021)

It was suspected trolls were responsible for getting him banned from DoorDash. He posted about his ban on Twitter stating, "When trolls say get a job they dont really mean it. I haven't door dashed in weeks. This is 100% troll stink." (Jordan, 2021) In the letter from DoorDash, which Jordan included in his Twitter post, it states, "We regret to inform you that your Dasher account has been deactivated. We received a report that you created an unsafe environment involving claims of discrimination and/or harassment towards another person while using DoorDash."

How trolls would get Jordan banned is not known for certain. If the trolls were responsible, it was speculated they used the fact that Jordan had discussed a customer on stream. Because he used their real name (first name only), he was reported by trolls to DoorDash for giving out customer information.

In July of 2022, Jordan deleted all his videos on his channel for the stated reason some troll was falsely copyright claiming them. This erased over a decade of work. This had numerous unintended consequences. The deletion of all those views tanked his remaining videos and channel in the YouTube algorithm. Any residual income from those videos was also destroyed. His archive of old content was likely lost to time.

The first real collaboration Jordan had in a long time was an influencer boxing match between Jordan and another creator, Boogie2988. They were both lolcows who caught the attention of Daniel Keem aka Keemstar. Keemstar even visited Jordan at his home in South Carolina to convince him to take part on April 14, 2023. It was jarring for many viewers to see someone be able to penetrate Jordan's usually reclusive life. The boxing event took place on May 13, 2023 in London, England.

Jordan easily won the fight and defeated Boogie2988 in a TKO in the first round. Jordan then quickly returned to South Carolina and continued on as usual. He continued collaborating with Keemstar with his *Lolcow Live* podcast. Keemstar offered Jordan a handsome salary and this kept Jordan coming back.

In March 2025, a significant controversy emerged during a livestreamed podcast/series called *Fat Camp*, which is part of *Lolcow Live*, co-hosted by Keemstar. During an episode, a physical altercation occurred between Jordan and Keemstar. (LolcowLive, 2025) As part of that altercation, which was probably scripted, Jordan pushed his wife, Kelly, when she attempted to intervene, knocking her on the ground. These moments provoked strong responses from viewers and fellow content creators. Jordan was trolled with names like "WingsofSpousal Abuse". Keemstar later announced that he was firing Jordan from his collaboration due to these incidents. Jordan was later invited back onto *Lolcow Live*.

As of writing, fall of 2025, Jordan is still streaming on YouTube and doing *Lolcow Live*. Amusingly, his channel banner is stuck in time and not updated. It features *The Podcast Show,* which stopped broadcasting eight years ago. His YouTube channel is stable at around 450,00 subscribers over the last two years (Social Blade, 2025). His streams usually secure 200-500 live viewers. His YouTube channel has an average of 1,500 to 1,800 daily viewers. For a channel of that subscriber size, it is generally seen as very low performing or a "dead channel".

Troll names:	**Troll Sayings:**
Wingo	"Big Ups, Liquid Richard"
Richard	"Shoutout Sean Ranklin"
Liquid Richard	"Look Here, look listen"
Jordan Samuel McGravy	"Brandy got blacked"
Plump Pimp	

Other memes:

Modular mansion: Jordan was often trolled because he lives in a mobile home. He was annoyed at people calling it a mobile home or trailer and continued to insist it was a "modular home". Trolls then started calling his house the modular mansion.

Wendy's chilli: Jordan is often trolled because he ate Wendy's chili. The trolls kept referencing it because it annoyed him.

Jordie Jordan did not respond to a request for comment.

You can use this QR Code to access Wings of Redemption's main YouTube channel:

You can use this QR Code to access an archived version of "wingsofredemption gets stream sniped and loses it" by Sean Ranklin:

Chapter 8: Boogie2988 aka Steven Williams

Boogie2988 was once called the "Mr. Rogers of the Internet" for his perseverance, after a difficult upbringing, and maintaining a hopeful outlook on life. The man behind it, Steven Williams, was once an inspirational figure and a huge creator on the platform. He made personal vlogs, video game commentary, and rant style content. However, Williams was soon unmasked. The man everyone thought they knew so well, was something much different.

Steven Williams was born in July of 1974 in St. Paul, Virginia. St. Paul is a small working-class Appalachian town. In archetypical fashion, Williams' father was a coal miner. Williams has discussed, at length, his childhood as abusive. His mother was erratic, and this resulted in Williams being physically assaulted to the point of causing permanent injuries.

Williams found solace in video games and food. This unhealthy relationship with food meant his weight quickly ballooned. Morbid obesity would be an issue that would follow him for the rest of his life. After high school, Williams briefly attended college but dropped out. What followed was a life of "drifting". He would work dead end jobs, couch surf at friends' apartments, and have little direction in life.

Williams started uploading YouTube videos in 2006, right when the website opened. The channel name, Boogie2988, was taken from his old gaming moniker. His early videos were vlogs, discussions about video games or *Magic: The Gathering,* and stories about his life. His first viral video "Dramatic Fat Guy Splash" was released on August 14, 2011. It shows Williams fall into a pool. Williams was around 500 pounds at this time. It currently sits at over 39 million views. (boogie2988, 2011)

The next big hit, and what Williams became most known for, was his "Francis" character in 2011. Francis was a satirical character based on the angry gamer stereotype. He released several Francis videos like: "Francis Rages - Where's My Goddamned Mountain Dews?", "Fat Guy Destroys Xbox", and "Francis Plays Magic the Gathering". These videos each have over 10 million views. The "angry gamer" genre was very popular in the late 2000s and early 2010s with other popular YouTubers like AngryVideoGameNerd, AngryJoe, and IrateGamer.

Williams also made videos discussing his private life. These videos documented his early childhood abuse, his experience with bullying, struggles with morbid obesity, and his time in young adulthood as a drifter.

The viral Francis videos and private life videos, in combination with his regular content discussing nerd topics, propelled Williams to 100,000 subscribers on March 9, 2012. This was a high number of subscribers at the time and according to Williams, put his channel in the top 1,500 channels on YouTube. (boogie2988, 2012) In a tearful celebration, Williams explains YouTube changed his life. He met his girlfriend, and soon to be wife, on YouTube. He met many friends on the site. And his friends and family back home were proud of his success on YouTube.

Williams' success continued, and he reached 500,000 subscribers on June 10, 2013. (boogie2988, 2013) In 6 months that doubled to one million subscribers on November 17, 2013, a very high number of subscribers for the time. (boogie2988, 2013)

Williams also got married in 2013 to Desiree "Dez" Williams and they frequently appeared in content together. At this time, Williams was very highly respected. People fell in love with his story and rooted for him as an underdog. And he was genuinely passionate about gaming and other nerd topics. Many people were able to identify with him because he was so down to earth and vulnerable with the audience.

At this point in his career, even when everything was riding high, you can start to see some of the parasocial nature of his content. In his video celebrating hitting 1 million subscribers Williams states, "When it's just me and you [the audience] in a room sitting and talking to each other, it's the best feeling in the world." (boogie2988, 2013) Except, there is no 2-way conversation. The video is him speaking into a camera. This would hint at some of the problems Williams has with how he treats the internet. He treats the internet like a friend or parasocial relationship. (See Lolcow Trait #1 – Parasocial Relationship)

Williams continued his rise. He reached three million subscribers on February 2, 2016. This placed him as the 387th most subscribed channel on YouTube, out of millions of YouTube channels. It put him in the top 0.01% of channels. (boogie2988, 2016). To try and put that into perspective, if you are in the top 0.01% income group in the United States, you would make at least 17 million dollars a year. (*Internal Revenue Service*, 2025) That doesn't mean Williams was making this much money, but if a businessman told you they were making at least 17 million dollars a year, you would think he was pretty successful. In terms of the YouTube success scale, Williams was similarly very successful.

At the height of his popularity, he won "Trendy Gamer of the Year" at The Game Awards in December of 2016 for his coverage of video game topics. (Osborn, 2016) He hit four million subscribers on June 8, 2017. (boogie2988, 2017) This was the peak of his success.

At the peak of this success, controversy started to follow Williams. When Williams was at Vidcon 2017, he was on a panel with Anita Sarkeesian. Sarkeesian, a prominent social justice warrior made famous by the Gamergate controversy, was perceived to be bullying Williams. Many online creators, knowing Williams had mental health struggles, came to his defense. This would be the height of his respectability on the internet. Over time, more creators turned against him.

Peak

Williams had struggled with his weight all his life and consistently weighed over 400 pounds for many years. He got gastric bypass surgery in August of 2017. This weight loss surgery was going to assist with Williams' final personal issue which had been with him all his life: his weight.

Overcoming his personal struggles was built into his brand from the beginning. Especially in the early years, he built his public image as an underdog. He promised to get better and do better. For a while, things were continually improving for him. Throughout the late 2000s and 2010s, he and his girlfriend got married, he had weight loss surgery, and his YouTube channel grew massively. And with that massive YouTube channel came financial security.

On December 19, 2017, he announced he was getting a divorce from his wife. after being together for seven years. He revealed his wife was tired of dealing with his chronic pain, morbid obesity, and other issues. Now that Williams was losing weight and recovered from his surgery, she no longer needed to take care of him. In the video, "It's true, wife and I are getting a divorce. Here's what next for us" (boogie2988, 2017), Williams portrayed the divorce as amicable. His wife also left public life altogether.

He had to continue on his journey without a tailwind of success. His channel peaked in subscribers. Now that he had the weight loss surgery, he would have to deliver on his promise to actually lose the weight. And without his wife to assist him, he would have to go it alone.

Complacency and Controversy

Due to the divorce, his uploads dramatically slowed throughout 2018 as his depression increased. Additionally, his wife used to assist in making videos. Without her help, this also slowed him down. Interest in his style of content was also waning. There was much more competition in the video game and *Magic: The Gathering* genre on YouTube. He used to get 300,000 to 1,000,000 views per video in years past. This went down to 150,000 to 250,000 views per video. (Joon The King, 2019)

Williams started diversifying. He began streaming on Twitch and doing paid promotions. Twitch streaming would present a different side of Williams. According to Williams, YouTube Boogie is the person I try to be and Twitch Boogie is the Francis version of himself. (Joon The King, 2019)

This decrease in uploads also coincided with a number of controversies. There were two major factors that contributed to Williams' controversy. The first was the squeaky-clean image Williams had cultivated. The second was Williams' constant need to have some kind of neutral position. When his neutral position received any level of backlash, he then felt the need to apologize and go back on what he said. Any level of pushback necessitated a response from Williams, either in video form or Twitter. These extensive apologies, turns of course, and promises to change and do better, compounded over time - where they essentially meant nothing. And these are over fairly minor issues or "non-troversies".

One June 19, 2018, Williams appeared on the very popular *H3H3 Podcast*. His podcast appearance was received well but it did bring some controversy when Williams stated he was in favor of same sex marriage but wasn't in favor of it being done "right now". He preferred to change opinion about it and then get it done in 10-20 years to avoid backlash. Williams received enormous backlash from gay fans, as well as others, because his overly neutral position made it seem like he really didn't care about being an "ally" to them. Gay fans, as well as others, felt that placating homophobes or those who wish to deprive them of their rights was not the right thing to do.

In the same podcast, Williams revealed that he was seeing a much younger woman - under 21. At this time, Williams would have been 44 years old. Internet detectives went to work on social media. They quickly found the woman whom Williams could have been alluding to. Williams had liked posts on her Twitter. She was a cam model and a member of a sugar daddy website. More digging found Williams' profile on this sugar daddy website under the moniker: "BeatenAndBruised". (Yes. That is what he chose his profile name to be.) On his profile, his banner reads, "people pleaser who needs to be pleased." (Joon The King, 2019) This would also emerge as a pattern for Williams, where he would use trauma and abuse he had suffered to bait sympathy from people.

These online detectives, or trolls, started messaging this woman. She made a response video. In her video, she portrayed the relationship as very brief and spilled the beans about Williams. She claimed the way he is online is not how he is in real life. She made allegations of verbal abuse and guilt trips from Williams to bend her to his will.

These revelations had confirmed what many online people suspected. His "nice guy" persona was an act. Let's pause here for a moment. Williams, who had enjoyed a very positive and wholesome public image, had been unmasked as a "sugar daddy". For many who maintained this wholesome image of him, it started to turn people away.

In October 2018, Taylor Lorenz, a well-known social justice warrior, wrote an article criticizing many YouTubers for promoting the service, BetterHelp. (Lorenz, 2018) BetterHelp is an online counseling service to help people with mental health issues. These influencers, including Boogie2988, would get referral bonuses for their fans who signed up.

This article got a lot of attention and pretty soon there was a backlash against creators promoting BetterHelp. Williams eventually caved to the pressure and dropped BetterHelp as a sponsor.

Williams was a figure in the *Magic: The Gathering* community. *Magic: The Gathering* is a strategy card game. Wizards of the Coast, the makers of the game, wanted to have Williams be a guest at a charity event they were running. Williams was friends with Jeremy Hambly, a fellow YouTuber who also made content around the card game. Hambly was previously banned by Wizards of the Coast from their events. In the video uploaded on October 22, 2018: "Boogie2988 Fired for Our Relationship" Hambly states in the video because Williams didn't disavow him; Williams was fired from the event, despite being a big draw. Even though Williams was fired from the event, he continued to do a separate charity event. He also apologized for not doing the Wizards of the Coast event. It wasn't clear what he was apologizing for.

Hambly states "My biggest complaint about him is of many the times, I believe, he's saying something he truly believes in he gets bullied into apologizing. But it's his life. It's his channel. It's his business. It's his brand. So ok. It's really not my concern." (TheQuartering, 2018)

This was a growing concern for Williams and his reputation as a "fence sitter". He would react to any controversy. Anytime he received pushback on anything, he would apologize or reverse course. This pattern can be seen in his podcast remarks about gay marriage, yielding to pressure to abandon sponsors, and apologizing for being fired.

When Williams was streaming on Twitch, he also let his mask slip. He would engage in toxic behavior including taunting teammates and make disparaging comments towards people in chat. Williams also began spending more time on Twitter. He would get into arguments with random people and then apologize for arguing with those people. (Joon The King, 2019)

Weaponizing Threats of Suicide

Vidcon is a YouTuber convention where creators and fans meet up annually. Williams attended Vidcon 2019 which ran from July 10, 2019 to July 13, 2019. Williams had been regularly attending Vidcon since 2014. He was featured in a keynote speech in 2017. Vidcon was a great marketing, networking, and a content creation opportunity for Williams and lots of other creators.

In his two vlogs that remain public from that Vidcon, "Rambling: I RUINED my feet at vidcon rofl…" and "LANCE STEWART CONFRONTS BOOGIE2988 AT VIDCON!" Williams discussed his time at Vidcon 2019. He says, "I had a really great Vidcon" in a video dated July 17,

2019. He continues by saying, "I was going into this Vidcon as it being my last Vidcon as a creator and with the intention of full-on retiring and quitting everything and just trying to figure out my life. But I'm going back home with a passion again." (boogie2988, 2019) Williams goes on to say, "I walked into this Vidcon nervous and anxious and sad and scared and I'm walking out of this Vidcon confident and happy and excited and ready to create content." (boogie2988, 2019) Everything seemed normal for Williams. These videos don't seem different from any of his other Vidcon videos.

While Williams projected outward normalcy to the audience, he presented himself much differently in person with other creators. When interacting with other creators he told them he was going to kill himself. When Williams met GamerFromMars, another creator who he had never met before, he introduced himself as, "Hello GameFromMars how's it going? To be honest, I've been thinking about killing myself." This was repeated by other creators that he met at Vidcon, including McJuggerNuggets and KidBehindaCamera. However, other creators thought it was just a joke. A twisted joke, but a joke. (Seethin Steven, 2024)

Williams, in a now deleted Tweet when referring to Kat Blaque, a fellow Youtuber, stated, "Kat you aren't special here. I was in desperate pain trying to find a way out. I told literally everyone within earshot at vid con that I was suicidal." (Williams, 2020) Additionally, in an episode of *Lolcow Live* in June of 2025 stating, "I just had to walk up to Hank Green and John Green and be like, 'So anyway I plan to delete myself [internet speak for suicide] after Vidcon and uh, would guys like to be nice to me? Can I manipulate you with this, please?' And they did not want to be manipulated." Hank Green and John Green were fellow creators that ran the popular YouTube channel Crash Course and SciShow.

(Seethin Steven, 2025) Also, they were the founders of Vidcon.

In that same *Lolcow Live* episode, the Billy of the Billy The Fridge YouTube channel states, "He must have done a suicide speech to like, in front of me, the same damn speech to like a dozen big YouTube people. It was the same speech. We would be walking around he'd be like, he'd find a big YouTuber and be like, 'Oh, you know, I'm going to kill myself.' And it was like 'What the heck?'." Williams chimes in and says, "I did it to Idubbbz." Idubbbz was a fellow creator that had four million subscribers at the time and was at the height of his popularity. (Seethin Steven, 2025)

Williams had another suicide controversy in July of 2019 where he wanted to match donations for suicide prevention. He then lowered his contribution to a max of $10,000. People complained $10,000 was a very small amount of his annual salary. When asked why he lowered this, the way he responded created more controversy. On Twitter he posted, "My original plan was to give it all away and kill myself. I have since decided that killing myself will hurt too many people so I am choosing to endure instead. Keeping some of my money to live on until I die. Sorry if that upsets you." (Joon The King, 2019)

Many people were shocked by his remarks and found it manipulative. In that post, he baits the viewer into sympathy because he is suicidal. Then, he plays the hero by deciding not to kill himself and carry on with living for the sake of the viewer.

Just when it couldn't get worse, Williams, in a Twitch stream, directed his anger at his detractors in response to his tweet. (Joon The King, 2019) He stated:

"They take something someone tweeted, something someone said, tries to make it look worse that it really is for the purposes of just destroying somebody's life [himself]. If you are this person, and you know who you are, it might be difficult to reconcile that you are that person. But if you are that person I ask you a favor: please keep doing it to me. Don't do it to other people. Let me be a martyr. Martyr me. I'm gonna stay online and I'm going to stay alive as long as I can. I'm gonna waste as much of your time as you can. I'm going to say as much s**t and do as much s**t as I can to keep your attention so you don't do it to somebody else. I'm here for you to torture me and only me. I'm gonna make a living letting you torture me. I'm going to be the next DarkSydePhil. I'm going to be the next WingsofRedemption. I'm going to spend every day online to keep you f**king busy so you don't do it to somebody else. So bring it. But I want you to know I think you are the lowest of the low. I think you are the worst of the worst. I think there are f**king rapists and Nazi's out there who, even though they are rapists and f**king Nazis, they are more redeemable than you because at least they're doing something they f**ing believe in."

He later doubled down on these statements on Twitter. But then walked them back in a YouTube video he uploaded in September 2019 stating that he was struggling with mental health issues which clouded his feelings. The reaction to this video was mainly negative. Viewers, expressing their feelings in the comments section, found him manipulative. If you read it, it doesn't sound like something the "Mr. Rogers of the Internet" would say.

By 2019, his channel had decreasing viewership, negative engagement, and was losing subscribers. His antics at Vidcon 2019 had also burned many bridges with other content creators.

The Shot Heard Around the Internet

Williams was involved with a verbal altercation with a known internet troll, Frank Hassle, on an internet web show called *Kill Stream* hosted by Ethan Ralph. Hassle and Williams verbally sparred over whether or not Williams was a manipulator, among other issues they had with each other. Hassle stated he would be traveling to Arkansas to film Williams.

Hassle, while in Arkansas, made a Tweet directed at Williams saying, "I'm in Fayetteville p**sy @Boogie2988". Keemstar, host of the web show *Drama Alert*, invited both onto the show. More verbal sparring ensued. Hassle said he would film outside Williams's house. Williams threatened to kill Hassle stating, "When you're laying dead on my f**king front lawn that won't be f**king funny" and later stated, "You know where I live Frank. I'm waiting. We're locked and loaded, show the f**k up." Hassle laughed at Williams in response. (Joon The King, 2023)

Hassle did show up at Williams' door in September of 2020. He filmed the encounter. Williams answered the door with a revolver in his hand. (Kluster, 2025)

"Is this what I have to do?" Williams asks, as he opens the door. Hassle laughs loudly. Williams appears to be serious.

"You fat f**k," Hassle replies. "Oh my God!"

"I'm asking you to leave," Williams states.

"Is this real?"

Williams repeatedly asks Hassle to leave. Hassle continues to laugh and taunt Williams. Williams states, "In 30 seconds I'm going to fire a warning shot."

"Fire it now!" Hassle replies.

Williams steps out of his doorway and onto his porch. He points the gun upwards and fires into the air. Williams continues to ask Hassle to leave. And Hassle continues to taunt Williams. Williams then points the gun directly at Hassle. (Hassle was unarmed.) Hassle does eventually leave.

Police investigated. And Hassle was not charged. The police issued an arrest warrant for aggravated assault against Williams on May 7, 2021. Williams turned himself in. Williams' defense was of castle doctrine. He feared for his life. He used the firearm in self-defense.

There were several *legal* problems with Williams' defense. (Let's think like a prosecutor here.) The first being Williams left his castle. He unlocked the door and stepped onto the porch to confront Hassle. If he was in fear for his life, why did he open the door? He should have kept the door locked and called the police. Secondly, there is no such thing as a "warning shot". In order for Williams to brandish and fire a gun, Williams would have to feel his life was in imminent danger. If Williams was in imminent fear of his life, why didn't he just shoot and kill Hassle on the spot? Third, Hassle was unarmed and simply knocked on Williams' door. Once he asked Hassle to leave, and Hassle didn't, Hassle was then trespassing. Williams should have called the police. The police would have removed Hassle from the property. Contrary to popular belief, you can't direct deadly force (brandishing and firing a gun) at someone else for simply trespassing.

After the encounter, Keemstar released the footage (Hassle had his YouTube channel removed before this.) The internet erupted in a fury of this latest controversy. It was the first time in internet history a creator had used a gun against a troll.

In May of 2022, Williams took a plea deal and avoided jail time but did become a convicted felon.

Broke

Williams began posting about his financial struggles on Twitter in 2019, as his views and revenue declined. In June of 2019, he discussed purchasing a Tesla. He posted his excitement about the vehicle, but then also about the financial hardship he would experience paying for it. This obviously turned more people off of his channel. He wanted to brag about his possible purchase, but he also put the burden of paying for this vehicle on the audience. Williams tried to explain himself on Twitch, "I tweeted out that I was not going to be able to afford this car. Reddit lost their f**king minds. *Oh, are you trying to manipulate people into giving you money.* The answer is yes. Give me some money." (Brighty Gamer, 2019)

Williams reversed course and claimed he was rich in a video he posted on January 18, 2021 titled, "I am Finally RICH - How Crypto Made Me Rich" (boogie2988, 2021) In the video, he states during 2019 when he had his mental breakdown and was threatening suicide, he invested all his money into the crypto market. He implies his money quadrupled in value from early 2020 to the present day.

On October 5, 2022, Williams made a video titled, "I need your help." (boogie2988, 2022). In the video, he announced he lost a lot of money in the cryptocurrency market. It would later be revealed he lost at least 500,000 dollars. This destroyed his nest egg. Williams also states because he uploads less videos his regular income decreased. This decrease was a result of both no new views and his enormous back catalogue of videos that had fallen out of the algorithm. Williams then asked for financial support from the audience.

This video propelled Williams as a topic for the YouTube commentary community. He was widely criticized and trolled for wasting his money. But, he still had some money, a massive YouTube channel, and was still able to make a living; just not at the level of lifestyle he had been accustomed to. Most people thought his video came across very tone deaf.

Williams appeared on the web show *Financial Audit* with Caleb Hammer on December 11, 2023. Hammer runs a personal finance channel that helps people with budgeting. The whole video is 1 hour and 38 minutes long. Williams explained his numerous financial difficulties. Hammer tried to help Williams with his crumbling financial position. I would recommend watching the video for full context. (Hammer, 2023)

After the episode, Williams went on to disparage Hammer on *Lolcow Live*. Hammer later recalled on a different podcast, *The Iced Coffee Hour,* on August 12, 2024, "He's interesting behind the scenes…The dude is just so nice and gentle in person and you can tell unlike you guys [referring to Graham Stephan and his co-host, Jack Shelby] you're the same as you are off camera. I think I'm the same off camera as I am on camera. He's not. He kind of puts on a show. Which is why I think a lot of people find him to be a little more fake which isn't surprising why an audience would fall like that." (The Iced Coffee Hour Clips, 2024) Hammer goes on to say, "After we recorded the episode and everything, he went on and trash talked on his podcast… He trash talked on Twitter.

And then a couple of times on Twitter he was like oh, this is for the drama. And it was very confusing to follow."

Hammer also adds, "One thing he's really good at, he's very good at the manipulation around therapy talk." Graham asks, "What is therapy talk?" Hammer explains, "Therapy talk in terms of just bouncing around subjects and making everyone feel very sympathetic for your situation and just making it seem like everything's excusable in a way. He was very good just dancing around things and also, I mean, he lied a lot as well." Hammer went on to say that Williams lied about his spending and made excuses for things. (The Iced Coffee Hour Clips, 2024)

The Dark, Sad Life of Boogie2988

The Dark, Sad Life of Boogie2988 was released on October 31, 2023 by independent filmmaker Mike Clum. Currently, the video sits at over 6 million views. I don't want to go through every detail of the documentary, because I think it is worth watching in its entirety. (Clum, 2023) The documentary put a spotlight on Williams at his lowest point. He was financially desperate. Williams also talks about his failing health. He sabotages a job interview with a work agency. It presents Williams as possibly having pathological tendencies like covert narcissism aka vulnerable narcissism. There were also new revelations about Williams' exorbitant spending on prostitutes. Having sex with Williams was so traumatic for one prostitute it compelled her to stop doing sex work and go back to school.

The internet erupted on release of the documentary. Williams was once again propelled as a topic of discussion and received some newfound relevancy. But it was mainly people criticizing him for his wasteful spending, sexual exploitation, and manipulation.

There were some good things which came out of the documentary. He was dating a much younger woman, Deziree (not to be confused with his first wife). He also got lots of new attention, allowing Williams to join a podcast called *Lolcow Live*. The money he was able to use from that show kept him financially afloat.

Faking Cancer

Williams released a video on November 15, 2022, titled, "I have a rare form of cancer." where he claimed he had cancer. (boogie2988, 2022) Another controversy erupted around Williams when he was promoting a cryptocurrency called "Faddy Coin". This was coming from a guy who admitted he lost most of his money in cryptocurrency. When cornered by Coffeezilla, a fellow creator, on the controversy and why Williams was promoting this coin (which many people suspected was a scam) Williams implied he needed the money for cancer treatment. (voidzilla, 2024)

On July 10, 2024, Williams was confronted by Steven Bonell aka Destiny on *Lolcow Live*. (Destiny, 2024) Destiny asserted Williams didn't really have cancer. Williams tried to defend himself after the confrontation but did eventually admit he was lying about having cancer.

Aftermath

Williams' controversies, criminal conviction, and exposure as a manipulator has destroyed his reputation. He used to collaborate all the time. Due to his toxicity, no other YouTubers will work with him, except Keemstar and his show *Lolcow Live*.

He still uploads online on his main channel, mainly getting 10,000 to 50,000 views, as opposed to 300,000 to

1,000,000 views his peak. His subscribers peaked in 2021, at around 4.2 million. According to Social Blade, he loses about 10,000 subscribers a month and currently sits at 3.9 million. (Social Blade, 2025) By standard YouTube metrics, his channel is considered a "zombie" or "dead" channel.

Steven Williams declined a request for comment.

You can use this QR Code to watch one of Boogie2988's earliest viral videos, Dramatic Fat Guy Splash:

You can use this QR Code to watch one of Boogie2988's earliest viral videos, Francis Where Is My Mountain Dew:

You can use this QR Code to watch the Mike Clum documentary: The Dark, Sad Life of Boogie2988:

Chapter 9: Rekieta Law aka Nick Rekieta

Rekieta Law is an online legal commentary channel presented by Nick Rekieta. He started making YouTube videos on various legal topics as a hobby. Instead of dry legal coverage, Rekieta pioneered covering legal topics and cases as entertainment. His small channel became one of the largest legal channels on YouTube. However, as he rose in prominence, with the accompanying wealth and fame, he destroyed his channel and personal life in a drug and sex-fueled crash out.

He describes Rekieta Law as "a small law firm in Minnesota" and on his channel, he engages in "Law-splaining the interwebs". It's a playful way of saying he discusses legal topics, ongoing legal cases, and other legal issues in a way to be approachable, informative, and entertaining to a general audience. Rekieta was an early pioneer of the "Law Tube" genre on YouTube and (at the time) was a licensed attorney.

Rekieta operates out of the small town of Spicer, in a rural area of Minnesota called Kandiyohi County. According to his LinkedIn, he went to college at Southwest Minnesota State University and got a B.A. in Literature and Creative Writing from 2001 to 2005. He then worked as a bank teller at Wells Fargo and then Thrivent Financial for Lutherans. He went back to school full time, from 2011 to 2015, and got his law degree from Mitchel Hamline School of Law. (Rekieta, 2025) It is unclear how he supported himself during his time in law school. At this point, he was already married with children.

Upon graduating from law school, he started Rekieta Law in 2015. Rekieta was admitted to the bar, according to MN records, on May 8, 2015. Rekieta Law's first Facebook post announced the opening of his firm on July 30, 2015. So, we can assume that is when Rekieta Law, the law firm (not YouTube channel) began. Later posts show a small physical office which opened. (Rekieta Law, 2025) This small office was located in a strip mall in the neighboring town of Willmar, MN, off the main road. This office must have closed at some point. Google Street View still has his law firm occupying that building in August of 2018 but by 2022, it is no longer there.

It is difficult to discern exactly how much law he actually practiced. According to the Minnesota Court Records Online website, a government website, he has represented 28 cases from 2015 to 2024. Most are family and criminal cases, but also a few civil cases. These are just cases in court; he could have been hired on legal matters outside of court.

His first case which went to court was in July of 2015 and was a child support case. In December of 2015, he worked a criminal case of receiving stolen property. In 2016, it was a more prolific year, he handled 7 cases, including felony criminal cases, estate, and custody. This continued until 2019. Around this time, Rekieta's YouTube career was in full swing and the number of cases his legal practice took up declined.

Arguably, the largest case of Rekieta's law career was his criminal defense of Melanie Beth Daniel which began in December of 2019. Daniel was accused of embezzling half a million dollars from two local businesses, eventually causing the business to go under. Daniel was facing 50 criminal charges, mainly felony theft. Of all those charges, 45 were dismissed, and 5 were convictions. This case made a few local papers. It was the only case Rekieta handled as an attorney (I could find) which was covered by the press. I reached out to Daniel to request her opinion on her legal representation, but she did not respond.

He handled one case in 2020, 2021, and 2024. His last case was a traffic charge against his mistress, April Imholte. He did not show up to court. She was subsequently convicted.

The exact date is unknown, but due to his ongoing legal drama, people went to the MN lawyer directory and found his license to practice was suspended. This was reported in September 2024. The last payment due for bar association fees was November 2024. As of writing, Rekieta has not reinstated his law license.

I researched six law firms in Rekieta's area which practice similar law and were sole proprietors or two person firms. I was surprised by the number of firms in such a rural area.

Firm	Attorney	Years of Experience as of 2019	Number of Cases 2015-2019
Rekieta Law	Nicholas Rekieta	4	26
Clayton Law Firm	Leeann Clayton	28	18
M&D Mack Daby aka New London Law	John Mack	50	162
	Ralph Daby	33	54
Daniel Mohs & Associates	Daniel Mohs	35	200+
Dawn M Weber Attorney at Law	Dawn Weber	19	150
Jones & Patock PA	Theresa Patock	23	200+

Cletus J Frank Law Office	Cletus Frank	28	68

Some of these firms don't even have websites and they most far exceeded the number of cases Rekieta handled. I spoke with Andrew Esquire aka Legal Mindset, a fellow LawTuber, asking his opinion on the number of cases Rekieta handled. He advised you can't judge a firm based on number cases alone. There are other factors like the complexity of a case. Additionally, a firm may handle legal matters which never see a courtroom.

There are two unique aspects to his legal career. The first being, he is a Creative Writing major. The second being, he started his own firm directly out of law school.

Being an English or social science major before going to law school is not that uncommon. But what is unique is Rekieta's interest in Creative Writing and Literature, which must have impacted his decision to start a YouTube channel. In my opinion, the technical aspects of the law are not really featured in his content. Reviewing case law, going over statutes, and reading the legal documents are not featured as much as his argumentation, creative legal theory, and rhetoric. And for the purposes of YouTube, those things are more interesting to an audience. As we will see later in this chapter, his lack of experience and technical knowledge of the law are his limitations.

It is very rare that someone who just graduated from law school would start their very own firm. I reached out to a number of LawTubers and asked, "Is it common to start your own practice directly out of law school?" One replied, "almost unheard of." And that you would need "daddy's money" to be able to do something like that.

It is more typical to start working as an associate attorney in private practice, in the public sector, or as in-house counsel at a large corporation. You can learn and gain experience under the supervision of more experienced attorneys.

There are many roadblocks you face starting a law firm right out of law school. You have a massive disadvantage to prospective clients because you don't have any experience. If there are high stakes, like money or jail time, most people (and myself) would want someone who isn't going to be learning on the job. As a new attorney, you don't have any real work experience. There are varying opinions on how much law school *actually* prepares you for working in a real legal field, especially a law field which requires going to court. It is possible to start your own firm right out of law school, but just takes a lot of work. You have to run a business and operate as a lawyer at the same time. Rekieta never had a paralegal to help him with his law practice during this time.

This chapter began with an overview of Rekieta's actual law practice because it does not get enough attention online. Rekieta draws upon his credibility as a lawyer to give legal commentary on his YouTube channel. His time as a lawyer is fairly low key, if being generous. Many would consider his law career to be mediocre or unimpressive. The most cases he ever handled in a year were seven. While he was able to secure several dismissals, I wasn't able to find a case where one of his clients were acquitted or went to jury verdict.

Rekieta as a Youtuber

Rekieta began making YouTube videos in 2017. (Rekieta Law, n.d.) His first videos focused on internet-related lawsuits, like Maddox and Dick Masterson, and other online creators' legal issues. He combined legal analysis with humor. His "small town" lawyer persona also made him endearing and approachable.

He continued to make these videos with a few thousand views. In 2019, his first really popular videos emerged covering the Vic Mignogna #MeToo allegations and lawsuit. Mignogna is an anime voice actor and well known to anime/animation fans. Around this time, the Me-Too movement was in full swing. Mignogna was the subject of an allegation of sexual harassment. Mignogna was fired from Funimation, and two other voice actors supported the Me-Too allegations against him. Mignogna filed a defamation lawsuit against them.

Rekieta soon became a source of information for people wanting to learn more about the lawsuit. Other parties wanting to learn about the lawsuit, including media outlets reporting on the story, frequently mentioned Rekieta's coverage since he was a lawyer. Rekieta also became a kind of spokesman for the case and defending Mignogna. Rekieta was so involved with the suit he started a legal fund for him. Rekieta also was able to interview Mignogna and recommended a lawyer to Mignogna to handle the defamation case: Ty Beard. Who is Ty Beard? Beard was a lawyer Rekieta knew in Texas, as Rekieta was originally from Texas. Beard is the lawyer in charge of Rekieta's family trust. According to the firm's website, Beard's specialty is in business planning, mergers and acquisitions, and tax/estate planning. (Beard & Harris Attorneys at Law, 2025)

Beard's representation of Mignogna was widely criticized for numerous procedural failures, like submitting paperwork late and lack of professionalism. (Cushing, 2022) For example, the court had to reject affidavits because they were improperly notarized. Beard had notarized them "based on a telephone call" which he did not know was actually a violation of Texas notary laws. When your lawyer doesn't know what the law is, it's a bad sign. It is possible that Beard is a competent attorney who was just totally out of his depth as he was not experienced with defamation cases. Mignogna lost the lawsuit and it cost him a great deal of money. After losing appeals, Mignogna was personally responsible for $283,000 in the other party's legal fees. (Cushing, 2022)

It's important to stop and pause here for a moment. Rekieta's lack of experience and technical knowledge of casework and the law had real world consequences for Vic Mignogna. Now, it is not fair to say that Mignogna didn't have the free will to choose whatever lawyer he wanted. But what experience or knowledge regarding defamation cases does Rekieta have? Rekieta wasn't licensed to practice law in Texas. He was a strip mall lawyer in rural Minnesota. In my research of Rekieta's actual representation, I wasn't able to find a case where he represented anybody as a plaintiff or defendant in a defamation case. Yet, he was comfortable providing legal recommendations to someone on that subject. And why would Ty Beard take a case in a legal field he doesn't report to be proficient/a specialist in?

Rekieta created a GoFundMe for Mignogna's legal defense. According to the GoFundMe page, all that money would be sent to his friend, Ty Beard, for legal expenses. Rekieta raised $261,200 from 6,600 supporters as of November 14, 2019. (Featherly, 2019)

With all that money being raised, was this even about the merits of Mignogna's case? Was this lawsuit about something else? Is it possible Rekieta manufactured outrage over Mignogna's #MeToo cancellation to then fundraise a legal fund which would be paid to his friend (Beard)? Would Rekieta have been so outspoken about and fundraised for the case, if the legal fund were paid to a different attorney, and not his friend? There were also rumors Beard funneled much of the legal work to Rekieta. I reached out to both Rekieta and Beard. They did not respond to a request for comment on the Mignogna case.

There is a clear distinction between providing legal commentary and providing legal advice. Commentary is just that - entertainment. Legal advice has real world consequences in real world cases. And as we will see later, this exposed some of Rekieta's limitations: his limited experience and knowledge of the law.

While the case was a massive failure for Mignogna, it was a massive win for Rekieta. Rekieta was able to gain significant viewership and audience from his coverage of the Mignogna case. Rekieta would go on to cover another large trial: the case of Kyle Rittenhouse in 2021.

The trial of Kyle Rittenhouse was a national story. The central question of the trial was if Rittenhouse acted in self-defense or cold-blooded murder? There was again another large political element (for context) of this case - the Black Lives Matter protests. These protests erupted into rioting in many cities. At one of these riots, Rittenhouse shot two people. He was later found not guilty by a jury.

Rekieta began covering the case. He strongly argued Rittenhouse was acting in self-defense and that his prosecution was politically motivated. Rekieta *again* became a source for people seeking legal information about the case. And again, Rekieta was able to secure an interview with Rittenhouse, just like with Mignogna. Fortunately, for Rittenhouse, the defense attorney handling his case wasn't recommended by Rekieta.

Rekieta also started discussing this case with other online lawyers and created a web of creators which became known as *Law Tube*. Rekieta was usually the largest channel to take part in any of these discussions. The Rittenhouse case, being much larger than the Mignogna case and well-covered in the media, helped Rekieta gain a large audience. Around this time Rekieta stopped taking new cases in his law practice and focused on his YouTube career.

His decision to focus on YouTube turned out to be the right move as Rekieta's popularity *exploded* due to his coverage of the *John C. Depp, II v Amber Laura Heard (2022)* trial.

Depp v Heard was another national headline case. It was a defamation case. Depp alleged that Heard's Me-Too allegations were false and cost him his lucrative acting career. He sued Heard for defamation alleging $50 million in damages. Heard countersued, claiming Depp defamed her. She alleged $100 million in damages. (Rosenblatt, 2022)

The case and Rekieta's coverage of the case became lightning in a bottle. The trial was something out of a movie, with various twists and turns, spellbinding testimony (including by celebrities), and other shocking revelations. People wanting to learn more about or follow the case did so through Rekieta's channel.

Rekieta skyrocketed in popularity. His videos went from 10,000-20,000 views to millions of views. His livestreams were very successful with nearly 100,000 live viewers. He also became one of the biggest recipients of super chats on YouTube. And in addition to the booming business, he was also making tons of connections. Other lawyers starting YouTube channels were platformed by Rekieta. Many lawyers, who were content creators, and were already active on YouTube also joined in on Rekieta's streams. Law Tube was officially born, and Rekieta was at the center of it.

It's hard to state how big Rekieta was at this point in his career. In five years, Rekieta went from being a strip mall attorney in rural Minnesota to one of the most well-known and respected lawyers on YouTube. He had a worldwide audience of people and loyal fans who tuned in to his streams to hear his legal opinions.

Many of Rekieta's loyal fans followed him off YouTube and on to more monetizable platforms. In the summer of 2022, Rekieta started a Locals account. Locals is a Patreon-like site where you can directly support a creator and be let into an exclusive club. In exchange, supporters can get exclusive content and access to the creator. It was reported Rekieta had over 5,000 monthly supporters. At an average rate of $5 per month, that would have netted Rekieta $25,000 per month. In 2023, Rekieta signed an exclusivity agreement with Rumble. Rumble is a video hosting site and competitor to YouTube. Rekieta's profile was so high that the CEO of Rumble, Chris Pavolvski, made a public statement announcing his arrival on the platform stating, "Rekieta is popular for his entertaining and insightful commentary, and we are proud to serve as the platform where he is free to be himself." (Rumble, Inc., 2023)

The exact dollar amount was not known, but many have speculated his exclusivity deal was worth up to six figures.

Mask Off

In Rekieta's early streams, he closely guarded information about his personal life and family members. This is a reasonable move because the internet is a harsh place. As a public figure, it is best to have some degree of separation, but this policy of privacy and separation did not last. By 2022, aspects of Rekieta's life began to become public knowledge. It is unknown why Rekieta changed his policy on sharing personal details. It's possible he felt emboldened by his newfound fame.

In 2022, at the height of his popularity, the controversies began to pile up. These controversies were not related to his legal commentary, but his personal life. In October of 2022, his Locals chat became a forum for sharing nudes and other private photos. Rekieta would not discourage the posting of "private content" but rather branded his Locals chat as "free speech" and "censorship free". This resulted in many female audience members posting racy images in the Locals chat. Rekieta began engaging with these people, instead of moderating them out of the community. (Waifu, 2019)

There were additional photos provided by Nick and his wife, Kayla. Kayla posted lewd photos. Nick posted a photo of a liquor bottle in between his butt cheeks. This was later explained away as a "joke" and just humor which had gotten out of hand, when he was later confronted. Kayla made posts in Locals defending her photos that there was nothing wrong with what she was doing and she was "proud of her body". (Waifu, 2019)

In August of 2022, Rekieta announced he was taking his wife to Jamaica. Later, nude pictures they posted to Locals, and various details he let slip in streams, allowed people to locate the resort as Hedonism. On the Hedonism website, it describes itself as *"an all-inclusive, adults-only, clothing optional resort where inhibitions can be left at the door and the thrill of discovery awaits around every corner. Immerse yourself in an exotic escape."* (Hedonism II, 2025). You get the idea, it's a sex resort. There is wife swapping, hooking up, sex themed and risqué parties, etc. He would later admit to being at the resort.

In November of 2022 and into February of 2023, Rekieta posted videos which were essentially an endorsement of a male sex toy called the Balldo. I will spare you the details of what a Balldo is. Nobody had ever heard of the Balldo, until Rekieta introduced it to the general public. Many memes have spawned from his Balldo affinity, including Rekieta being known as the "the Balldo man" or simply, "Balldo". And his home is now referred to as the "Balldo Bunker".

In December of 2022, Rekieta also discussed in his streams about going to an "underwear bar" for his birthday with his wife. This bar, Gay 90s, is a known LGBTQ bar.

Needless to say, all of these controversies were upsetting his regular audience. Rekieta had mainly cultivated a politically and socially conservative audience. He portrayed himself as a traditional father of five homeschooled children, and he was active in his church. He publicly stated he and his wife were virgins until they met each other. In his early career, stated they were totally monogamous.

He was also streaming and uploading less frequently. He had left the peak phase of his channel and transitioned into the stagnation phase. As more and more of his audience left, there was nobody coming in to replace them.

Sometime in October of 2023, Rekieta met April and Aaron Imholte. Aaron was a fellow content creator and local to the area. He ran an internet show called *The Steel Toe Morning Show*. (The show's logo is a steel-toe boot.) They began socially engaging and were frequent guests at the Rekieta house. The Imholtes made appearances on Rekieta's show.

In January of 2024, there was the infamous hot tub stream. The Imholtes and the Rekietas (Nick and his wife) appeared on a live stream in a hot tub. They had obviously been drinking. The stream feels *off*. Everyone seems like they are overly familiar and inappropriate. It also includes Nick playfully touching Aaron Imholte. This fueled many rumors the Rekietas and the Imholtes were *swinging*.

Going into 2024, Rekieta's position did not improve. He began streaming less and less and his audience grew tired of his debauchery. And when I say streaming less, he would go weeks at a time without streaming, where in the past he would stream three to five times a week. Rekieta began to spiral out of control and continued drinking heavily and showing up late to streams. His views declined, engagement shrank, and the super chats dried up. He officially entered the creator's decline phase.

Due to Rekieta's antics and fall from grace, he was voted "Lolcow of the Year" in January 2024 (Lolcow of 2023) by Kiwi Farms, an internet forum site. Rekieta began lashing out at Kiwi Farms. Many of his shows became reacting to "trolls" on the Kiwi Farms and defending his bad behavior. His feuding with Josh Moon, owner of the site, and the Kiwi Farmers (what posters on the site are called) became featured more and more in his streams. There was no longer any "law" in his content.

This brings us to April of 2024 and Rekieta's last case as a practicing attorney. Rekieta was the attorney for April Imholte for a traffic violation. Her hearing date was set for April 23, 2024. It was a virtual hearing. Rekieta did not appear at the virtual hearing. April, who was not required to appear as long as her attorney appeared, was also not present Because neither of them showed up, April was convicted. Rekieta later stated he was sick and unable to make the hearing.

House Raid

Suddenly, everything would come crashing down around Rekieta. Just as Rekieta's career was in shambles, so was his home life. The police received reports of child neglect from a mandatory reporter at the Rekieta's church. Per the search warrant, "It was reported from a church preschool teacher that the children had complained of being hungry, not being fed, and wearing the same clothes for 3 to 4 days at a time and would start to smell. Nicholas was reported to being lethargic and appeared high or drugged driving a car around."

They began to research Rekieta and, being a public figure, they began watching his streams. This provided police with vital evidence. To quote from the search warrant, "In videos from January 2024 compared to May 2024, Nicholas appears to have lost weight, appears tired, and overall appears 'strung out', common with controlled substance users."

The warrant later goes on to cite a specific incident which served as the probable cause to search the home for evidence of child neglect:

> "The video is from 5/21/2024 and is of Nicholas in his basement studio talking about a court appeals ruling he lost. He appears in the video to be drinking alcoholic beverages and eventually appears under the influence of a substance or substances. The entire video blog is 4 hours and 4 minutes long. Approximately 2:46 into the video, Nicholas leaves to go to use the restroom. When he returns at 2:50:40, he appears to be making an excited look and has a white powdery substance on his nose. Your Affiant

believes his behavior is indicative of Central Nervous System Stimulants. Your Affiant believes based on training and experience as well as the behavior of Nicholas, that he ingested this white powdery substance through his nasal cavity while off camera. Your Affiant knows through training and experience that ingesting controlled substances through a nasal cavity is common amongst controlled substance users and is often referred to as 'snorting'. Your Affiant also noted that throughout the video, Nicholas is so under the influence of a substance to the point he has to close one eye to read his screen, rambles, and slurs his speech. Nicholas would obviously not be able to care for his children in this state of intoxication"

On May 23, 2024, the police raided his home. What the police uncovered was a house of horrors. I won't go through the whole transcript of the bodycam footage, but the whole house was in disarray. Clutter, dirty laundry, and garbage filled the house. Drug paraphernalia was out in the open. Liquor bottles were everywhere. And the police were able to locate controlled substances which were later confirmed to be cocaine, digital scales, as well as credit cards and money with white powdery substances on them. Needless to say, Rekieta, Rekieta's wife, and April Imholte, who was living at the house, were all arrested and the Rekieta children taken away by Child Protective Services.

Obtaining the bodycam footage has been its own legal battle. But the notes taken by those who saw the bodycam footage are reference material everyone has used to visualize the event. The following is taken directly from the notes (SWC Backup, 2025):

Pomplun [the officer in charge of the investigation] asks Nick, "We want to ask you some questions…a quick interview. We want to get an idea of the layout of the house, where the nanny is at, and who all stays here."
Nick immediately pushes back and asks, "What's your probable cause?"
Pomplun replies, "You have the search warrant."
Nick stands there with his arms crossed. He's calm, but he looks like s**t. He says, "Cool. You have no probable cause."
Pomplun asks, "Are you willing to talk with me?"
Nick responds, "Sure," then immediately adds, "You still have no probable cause."
Pomplun says, "I'm not discussing that. You've been given the search warrant. You know how this works."
Nick again says something about probable cause.

Rekieta's behavior during the raid was highly criticized. He was belligerent, childish, and uncooperative. Upon receiving a copy of the warrant, he throws it on the ground. He also hurled insults at the police. While Rekieta was being led away in the police car, he shouted at the police, "I hope you get gonorrhea and die." His performance as a lawyer was lackluster. Despite telling listeners to his show to *stop talking* and *invoke your 5th amendment right against self-incrimination* when questioned by the police, Rekieta *waived* his 5th amendment rights and continued to speak with them.

Law Tube v. Rekieta

Just as Rekieta had covered other people's legal issues, the internet jumped at the opportunity to cover his case. His arrest was even covered by the local Minnesota press. Just as Rekieta had been fading away into obscurity, these legal matters propelled him to the front page of Law Tube. Most Law Tubers weren't small-time creators Rekieta had to platform to get attention anymore. While Rekieta had been faltering and fading, these other Law Tubers were gaining market share. They had their own audiences and had been studiously developing their channels.

As legal commentators, they began to review the legal documents about Rekieta's case. Many were also friends or acquaintances of Rekieta and were predisposed to being sympathetic to him. But as the details of child neglect and substance abuse came to light, many broke contact with him.

The main consensus, with few exceptions, across all Law Tubers was Rekieta should shut up, seek rehabilitation, strike a plea deal because he was a first-time offender, and move on. "Move on" was defined as repairing his relationship with his family and/or returning to his core business to support his family - making content again.

Rekieta's reaction to being raided by the police was described by commentators as a "crash out". He became immediately hyper defensive about the situation.

Two future revelations further isolated Rekieta: the notes describing the body cam footage of the raid on his house and drug tests indicating Rekieta's nine-year-old daughter tested positive for cocaine with a hair follicle test. (MNPublicRecords, 2024) Rekieta disputes the description of the body cam footage and the accuracy of the hair follicle test.

A transcript of the bodycam footage of the police raid was put online. A local woman, who goes by the moniker: Momma K, went to the Kandiyohi County Courthouse and wrote detailed notes while watching the video. Rekieta responded to this on Twitter by claiming that Momma K was an "obsessive weirdo" and "She should be put down."

Rekieta's very aggressive reaction to criticism was a standard operating procedure for him. (Rekieta Law, 2025)

Rekieta and Alcohol

Rekieta's first videos, I believe, were filmed at his physical office location at the strip mall. In his first video, that is still public on YouTube, "Rekieta Law Breakdown: Maddox v Dick Masterson #2", alcohol is featured in the first 15 seconds of the video. (Rekieta Law, n.d.) On his Twitch channel, which doesn't have any public videos, he describes himself as a "Small Town Minnesota Lawyer with a lot of whisky and rage to make it through the stupidity". (Rekieta Law, 2025)

From the very beginning of Rekieta's online career, alcohol was featured prominently. To be clear, in his early videos he did not appear drunk or heavily inebriated. In these videos, whiskey was featured as a treat at the end of a hard workday. He would drink, unwind, and talk to the audience about legal topics. Over time, alcohol began to be featured more and more. He started doing whiskey review videos in 2021. And if you go to his channel and search for the word "whiskey", that word appears in the title of videos over 30 times and in the description of over 100 videos. (Rekieta Law, n.d.)

During his rise to prominence in 2019 through 2022, he began receiving lots of super chats from people who would super chat him to "toast". These toasts would be for past loved ones, getting a new job, birthdays, anniversaries, etc. and would be followed by a sip of alcohol, usually whiskey.

By 2023, his drinking increased. He regularly appeared on camera slurring words, losing focus, and acting strangely. He often trails off into a meandering soliloquy that appears to be an alcohol-induced ramble. These rambles also alienated many of his audience. For example, in one stream he criticized his church, including their production value, the singing, the liturgy, and basic tenets of the Christian faith. He admitted it was so boring he fell asleep and had to be woken up by his wife. Many in his audience were Christian and were attracted to his image as a humble Christian family man who was active in the church. Other drunken rants about other topics also turned off the audience.

His heavy drinking on stream culminated in the infamous May 2024 stream, which was the basis of the search warrant. But before this, there were other streams where Rekieta was so intoxicated he appeared rambling, haggard, and incoherent. He also almost falls asleep on stream. And worst of all, he appears to be pleasuring himself underneath the desk. He would later claim he was itchy and simply scratching himself. Drinking is no longer featured on his stream because it is a violation of his probation.

The Nose vs The Toe and Other Legal Battles

Aaron Imholte, having heard of the arrest of Rekieta and his wife, then made public statements and comments on the case. Imholte began a media tour. He went on numerous detractor channels giving interviews and began to spill the beans about Rekieta. Imholte told stories of drug use, wife swapping, cuckoldry, and other debauchery. He also confirmed he was divorcing April, and that she was living at the Rekieta house. April was living with the Rekietas under the auspices of being a "live in nanny", but was essentially Nick's mistress. These stories also include tales of child neglect, Nick's crippling alcoholism, and other shameful or embarrassing events at the Rekieta house. Imholte expressed regret at his actions in taking part in the whole affair.

Rekieta, having been exposed by Imholte, started a battle against him. This was dubbed by the internet: The Nose v the Toe. Rekieta has a prominent Roman nose. Aaron Imholte runs a morning show called *The Steel Toe Morning Show*. However, these battles with Imholte only fueled more media coverage of Rekieta since some were "legal battles" they were covered by Law Tube.

Rekieta went through Imholte's old episodes of his show and discovered Imholte appeared to be forwarding a compromising photo of his wife Kayla to a friend of his. To quote from the warrant:

> "A review of defendant's talk show from May 27, 2024, it shows defendant and G.B. [Aaron's friend] participating. The two of them talk about K.R. [Kayla Rekieta] and about her tattoos. Then defendant is seen scrolling through his phone and it looks like he is taking a screenshot and then tells G.B. to look at his phone. G.B. looks at his phone and says "I like tattoos more than I thought." Defendant then responds, "your boy didn't do too bad did he." K.R. is then talked about in an explicit manner. G.B. confirmed he received a nude photograph of K.R. from defendant on May 27, 2024 during the show. He described K.R. as standing completely nude with her breasts fully exposed. He further described a tattoo under K.R.'s left breast in the photograph. Later, law enforcement was able to confirm with K.R. that she did have that tattoo under her left breast. G.B. said he deleted the photograph after."

Kayla reported the incident to the police as revenge porn. Aaron Imholte was then investigated, arrested, and charged. Imholte accepted a plea deal, paid a fine of $50, and

Kayla was granted a harassment restraining order against him on April 10, 2025. (Potentially Criminal, 2025)

In addition to this legal issue, Rekieta began telling his own embarrassing, or what he thought were embarrassing, stories about Imholte. This ranged from touting his own sexual prowess with April (Aaron's now ex-wife), implying the two had homosexual relations where Imholte was the bottom, and allegedly hacking into Imholte's computer - exposing his internet porn search history and privileged communications between Imholte and his attorney. Imholte later stated the FBI was investigating. It was speculated that Imholte, while at the Rekieta house, logged into his Google account there. This was the opening Rekieta exploited. Rekieta denied ever hacking Imholte's computer.

Rekieta was invited as a guest speaker to Hackamania 2025. It is a comedy and internet drama convention. At Hackamania, Rekieta leaked Imholtes and his private messages. I don't want to share what those messages are. Many of these private messages contained embarrassing and sexually explicit details. This could have been seen as revenge porn because they include sexually explicit material that was released without consent for the purposes of humiliation.

Rekieta also showed up to Stoney's Bar, where Imholte is either a frequent patron or co-ownerr. Because of Rekieta's continued attacks on Imholte and showing up unannounced to his place of business, he filed his own harassment restraining order against Rekieta in August of 2025. Rekieta hired an attorney called Frank White. White's representation was criticized as lackluster and appearing unprepared, according to Law Tuber Sean Martin aka Potentially Criminal in his recap video. Sean is a practicing lawyer with experience working as a prosecutor and defense attorney. (Stallyn19, 2025) For example, when White asked a question to the witness and the witness began to answer, White objected to his own question. The judge appears confused and face palms in secondhand embarrassment.

Rekieta was also fighting for custody of his children and was in court for his ongoing drug possession charges. He did not decide to take a quick plea deal and wanted to fight a legal battle with Kandiyohi County.

In June of 2024, it was leaked by a member of the Kiwi Farms under the moniker "MNPublicRecords" that Rekieta's nine-year-old daughter had tested positive for cocaine ingestion with a hair follicle test. (MNPublicRecords, 2024) This again fueled a firestorm of media coverage around Rekieta. All of Law Tube as well as troll/detractor channels, and commentary channels covered the story. Rekieta began vigorously defending himself online and repeatedly claimed the test was not accurate.

Aaron Imholte was arrested for breaking his HRO that Kayla had against him. During a 10-year anniversary of Imholte's web show celebration at Stoney's Bar, one of the guest speakers Geno Bisconte, publicly insulted Kayla Rekieta. Because this was Imholte's event, despite Imholte not saying the words himself, he was sentenced on September 30, 2025 to 364 days in jail, but served 15 days. (Herren, 2025)

At his sentencing, Imholte spoke in his defense and said, "In 2023, I entered into a degenerate, toxic relationship that never should have happened. I regret it and have been going to therapy. I have become a Christian and have been redeemed by my savior, Jesus Christ. I want to teach my son to be a better man. Words cannot express how sorry I am [referring to his victim]. We loved each other at one time.

Those feelings were betrayed by my actions. Because of which I have had my faith tested, optimism challenged, and my reputation has been tainted. I've been laughed about and this is my reality. If the court shows me mercy today, Geno Bisconte will never work for me again." Spectators said that Aaron Imholte's final words were, "All praise be to Jesus Christ, may God have mercy on my soul." (Herren, 2025)

Aftermath

In April of 2025, Rekieta took a plea deal related to his drug possession charges. He was sentenced to five years of probation and other community service. The charges against April and Kayla were dropped. Many were hopeful, with this legal dark cloud behind him, Rekieta would be able to finally tell us how he really felt about the case. He might even apologize. And he was not able to do so prior because he feared it would be seen "legally" as an admission of guilt.

Since returning to YouTube, Rekieta has remained mostly irrelevant in the Law Tube space. He tried to re-capture his success with coverage of the Karen Reed trial throughout 2025. However, these livestreams only got 10,000-20,000 total views, as opposed to the 250,000 - 1,000,000 views he got during the Johnny Depp trial. (Rekieta Law, n.d.)

Commentators, like the popular web show *Kino Casino*, have speculated Rekieta is still using drugs after he appeared on stream in May of 2025 with blue fingers, strange voice changes, and sounds of heavy breathing or inhalation were caught on his microphone. (Kino Casino Clips, 2025) These could be considered an indication of *whippet use* or inhaling nitrous oxide. It creates a euphoric feeling and short high. It is also not detected by drug tests, which Rekieta is subject to as a condition of his parole.

On May 23, 2025, Rekieta appeared on a livestream called, "THIS LITTLE PIGGY: A Steel Toe Roundtable Discussion". The livestream was mainly discussing The Nose vs. The Toe saga. They are Anti-Aaron Imholte. They have also been dubbed "Balldo washers" by Rekieta detractors (A play on Rekieta's Balldo nickname). Karl Hamburger, from *Who are These Podcasts,* who was on the panel, is friends with Keanu Thompson. Thompson requested to be invited on and was accepted on to the show.

She knew Rekieta through a mutual friend. She also knew both Aaron and April Imholte. Keanu and her husband, Geno Bisconte, are comedians and did comedy at Imholte's bar. They also were previously socially friendly with the Imholtes. Also, Thompson had been in communication with April since the house raid.

Thompson challenged Rekieta's version of the events and narrative about Aaron and April. (Nobody Likes Onions, 2025) This challenge against him made Rekieta very upset. Only a few minutes in, he begins to fume, call Thompson names like "retard" and "bitch", and yells. Rekieta was yelling so loud it blew his microphone out. Thompson remained calm and pressed Rekieta. Rekieta continued to be irate. He also slipped up and revealed other embarrassing secrets about his life, like April was living at Rekieta's second house, he taught April how to do whippets (inhalation of nitrous oxide), he introduced other drugs to April, that he "loved" April, and Kayla was considering divorcing him. This confirmed many of the sexual rumors about April and Rekieta. Rekieta's reaction to Thompson's questions were seen by many as a crash out.

In a conversation with me, I asked, "Why did he get that upset?" Keanu Thompson replied, "He didn't like that I was talking to April. He's manipulative and emotionally abusive."

Rekieta continues to lash out at detractors and trolls. Anything which could be considered criticism doesn't escape his wrath. For example, elissa clips, a clipping channel featuring Rekieta and many of his "lowlights" was attacked by Rekieta. Elissa clips does not engage in commentary. These are only snippets of Rekieta's stream. She announced she was diagnosed with cancer. Rekieta's response was, "I don't know how to laugh harder at this" and sarcastically remarked he was, "sorry to hear that." He continued by stated, "I don't give a f**k about these people." and "...she's an evil bitch." Rekieta then walked those comments back and apologized. (elissa clips, 2025)

Rekieta's dramatic rise and fall from grace was meteoric and catastrophic. Legal Mindset, in a discussion with me, stated, "Nick is one of the most unfortunate cases on YouTube. He could have been on TV. He could have had Netflix specials." and "It's sad."

Nick Rekieta did not respond to a request for comment.

Troll names:
The Nose
The Law Pope (self referenced in good humor)
Balldo Man
Balldo

Other memes:

Balldo Bunker: A play on Rekieta's balldo affinity and "bunker" referring to his basement studio

You can use this QR Code to Rekieta's main YouTube channel:

You can use this QR Code to go to Rekieta's May 2024 stream which served as the basis for the search warrant. On the left, is the full video. On the right, is the clipped version.

You can use this QR Code to go to a comedic fan reenactment of the bodycam footage based on the bodycam transcript available:

Chapter 10: Ian Washburn aka iDubbbz

Ian Washburn aka iDubbbz was one of the top comedy creators on YouTube in the mid-2010's. He was a trailblazing YouTube commentator with his successful *Content Cop* series. He was known for his wit, edgy humor, and associations with other top YouTubers of his era. After a failed attempt to pivot to new content, he exists as a shell of his former self.

Ian Washburn was born in California in July of 1990. He graduated from CalState San Marcos with a degree in business management. (Graham Stephan, 2021) He worked menial jobs at GAP and Legoland. While he was in college, he started making comedy videos on YouTube with the moniker, Idubbbz. By the time he graduated from college, his YouTube career was successful enough to be his full-time job.

He started his YouTube channel in 2012 making Let's Play videos. He started branching out with other content like *Kickstarter Crap* in 2013, where he would review Kickstarter projects, using humor to critique and mock them. It was a popular series and is still available on his channel as of writing. He also started a series called *Bad Unboxing* where fans would send him strange and absurd items. (iDubbbzTV, n.d.) He would open them and react comedically. Many audience members sent items that were as absurd as possible to get a reaction from Washburn for the audience's amusement. These early series would prove quite popular for Washburn as he quickly started growing his YouTube channel.

Washburn created a series called *Content Cop* in late 2014. (iDubbbzTV, n.d.) He would perform in-character as an "internet policeman" and satirically critique other YouTubers on their content, behavior, controversies, and other internet drama. His targets included some of the biggest YouTubers of that era, like: LeafyIsHere, Keemstar, RiceGum, and perhaps most infamously Tana Mongeau. *Content Cop* featured adult humor. Washburn frequently said slurs (including racial), insults, and other edgy humor. Washburn balanced appearing as silly, whimsical, and unserious with addressing real issues and providing commentary.

For example, in the *Content Cop* of Tana Mongeau, released in February of 2017, (iDubbbzTV, 2017) Washburn was responding to Mongeau. She criticized Washburn for saying the n-word, believing it was inappropriate to say. Mongeau said if Washburn "broke both of his legs and lost all of his subscribers I would be genuinely happy." Videos quickly surfaced of Mongeau saying the racial slur herself and her defense of the saying word where she pleaded ignorance of its offensiveness.

Washburn made a *Content Cop* on her to highlight her hypocrisy. Washburn explains in the video that the context of words matter. He provides the example of reading Huckleberry Finn out loud, which does contain the n-word. His point is reading the word in a historical book is different from using it as a slur against someone. To quote him in the video, "We are very f**king stupid [as a society] to hold this word [n-word] to this colossally high standard, whereas every other slur can be used in a comedic sense or editorial sense but not this one because that one has history. Well guess what, f**king retards, all the others ones have history too." And later stated, "Either all of them are okay. Or none of them are okay."

Washburn, in the video, traveled to a Tana Mongeau fan meetup. There was a portion of the event where fans could take a photo with Tana. Washburn waited in line and was able to get in close for the photo. It appears Tana does not recognize Washburn. They pose for a photo. At that moment, when the normal phrase is "say cheese", Washburn puts his arm around her. He leans in, smiles, and shouts, "Say N*****r!" Tana fled the photo op and later described the experience as horrifying.

Washburn ends the video by saying: "It's either all okay or none of it's okay. It's important to remember if you ever mistakenly identify a word 'off limits'. No words are off limits. You're allowed to get offended by the words. And say, 'Oh, I didn't like that very much'. But for you to come at the person and say 'you're a bad person for saying this. You're a racist for saying this.' At the end of the day, everything's a choice. Black people can choose to get offended by black slurs. Asian people can choose to be offended by Asian slurs. White people can choose to get offended by black slurs. And Tana Mongeau can choose to get offended by black slurs. At the end of the day, it seems like white people are really just trying to make up for all the torment we've inflicted on black people. Well, keep at your crusade. I'm going to continue to act like they're normal human beings."

The debate about the distinction between *saying* slurs and *using* slurs is beyond the scope of this book. We will only focus on how as it relates to the topic at hand.

It should also be noted the historical context of this era of YouTube - the mid-2010s. Social justice warriors (SJWs) were left leaning progressives and feminists active online. SJWs wanted to police online content and remove or censor content they found "problematic". Usually, this problematic content they described as racist, sexist, homophobic, Islamophobic, transphobic, etc. This movement spawned a reactionary movement that wanted content to be laissez-faire and actively defended free speech, though some went even further. Many content creators wanted their content to be edgy. So it could stand out or flaunt what it considered the forces of censorship or convention. This was also a common contrarian take on slurs of that era. Louis C.K., the famous comedian, made a similar argument in his 2012 stand up special, where he discussed the slurs: f****t, c**t, and n****r.

Content Cop rocketed Washburn's main channel, IdubbbzTV, in popularity. Content Cop was immensely successful getting tens of millions of viewers per episode. He would regularly get millions of views on other videos. He amassed over five million subscribers by 2017, which is a very high number. He also made a diss track (a song insulting someone else) called Asian Jake Paul, in October of 2017, that amassed over 80 million views before it was taken down in 2023. It featured PewDiePie, the largest YouTuber of that era, Ethan Klein of H3H3, Jack Douglass aka jacksfilms, Erik Hoffstad of Internet Comment Etiquette, and HowtoBasic. All of which were very successful and there was frequent cross pollination between their audiences. He also frequently collaborated with Ethan Klein of H3H3. Both described it as not just a business relationship, but true friendship.

Washburn was one of the most well-known figures in the YouTube commentary community. At this point, he was at the height of his career.

The Wild West Era was Over

Pre-2017 YouTube were the last days of the site's Wild West era. (People who were active on that site know what I'm talking about.) I remember being able to find full movies and television shows on YouTube, just split up into 10-minute sections. There was "adult content" on YouTube. You could upload street fights. People would upload videos of them getting into chases with the police. There were also channels that pushed conspiracy theories. There were dangerous pranks or challenges you should not attempt. You could do or say anything you wanted. And the whole site was much edgier due to a lack of moderation and enforcement.

A common misconception about YouTube is the viewers or creators are the customers of YouTube. No, the customers of YouTube are advertisers; Advertisers buy ads, creators make content, YouTube puts the ads in the creator's videos, and YouTube and the creators split the money. In the Wild West analogy, YouTube is the railroad. And the creators' YouTube channels are the towns and cities along the railroad. Both are dependent on each other. The creator is dependent on YouTube for video hosting, driving viewers, and monetization of their channel. YouTube is dependent on creators for making content. Without content, there's nothing to put ads on. However, there is a massive disparity in power between any one channel and YouTube. This means that YouTube can "railroad" any creator.

Just like the Wild West, with families moving in, advertisers got spooked by the edgy content and they began to pull out of YouTube. This resulted in a tumultuous time on YouTube called "the Adpocalypse". This is when advertisers pulled ads resulting in lost revenue for both YouTube and the creators. These Adpocalypse*s* ran from 2017 to December of 2019. As controversies from YouTube erupted, many of them not even the YouTube platform or creator's fault, YouTube had to convince advertisers to come back. And just like the end of the Wild West, this meant YouTube needed to have stronger law enforcement to end the lawlessness. Many creators disliked the loss in advertising revenue and were in favor of the reforms or saw them as inevitably necessary. Other creators wanted to preserve the laissez-faire status quo to protect freedom of expression. Well, money talks.

YouTube bent the knee to advertisers, and the creators were going to get "railroaded" by YouTube.

In December 2019, YouTube updated their community guidelines. These guideline changes tightened the standards around all sorts of content. YouTube staples like dangerous challenges and pranks were now off limits. This could have been in response to the shooting of Pedro Ruiz, a YouTuber making content with his girlfriend. They were filming a video to see if a book could stop a bullet. And needless to say, it could not, and Ruiz died of a fatal gunshot wound. (BBC, 2018)

YouTube increased regulations to prevent online bullying and harassment. In a post, YouTube stated, "Harassment hurts our community by making people less included to share their opinions and engage with each other". (DeFranco, 2019)

YouTube would take a stronger stance against threats and personal attacks. YouTube also stated, "We will no longer allow content that maliciously insults someone based on protected attributes such as their race, gender expression, or sexual orientation. This applies to everyone...". (DeFranco, 2019)

What are the consequences of breaking these new rules and guidelines? YouTube could suspend a creator from the YouTube Partnership Program. They would not be able to make money anymore. YouTube also stated, "They could also remove content from channels if they repeatedly harass someone. If this behavior continues, we will take more severe action including issuing strikes or terminating a channel altogether." (DeFranco, 2019)

This announcement caused massive waves in the online creator space. "#youtubeisoverparty" was even trending on Twitter. (Donna, 2019) People who disagreed with the additional regulations were free to go. They could go to alternative sites or start their own site. That was the norm pre-YouTube. And there were competitors to YouTube by this point. However, despite the complaints of additional regulation almost all creators stayed on YouTube because it was the only game in town.

Because Washburn's content was so volatile he was immediately impacted by these new rules. *Content Cop* ran afoul of the new harassment guidelines. Washburn's best performing video series went the way of the American buffalo. In December of 2019, YouTube removed his *Content Cop* video about LeafyIsHere. (H3 Podcast, 2019)

Seeing the writing on the wall, Washburn decided to retire *Content Cop* and moved on to other projects. These other projects included his *Bad Unboxing* series, which still got millions of views and his channel was still riding high.

He branched out into long form content. He created an hour long documentary about Airsoftfatty, an early viral YouTuber. He is an overweight man who made lightsaber fight videos in his yard. The reaction to the documentary was mixed. Some thought it was incredibly funny and entertaining, while others thought it was exploitative, mean spirited, and/or awkward. But the video got massive views, currently sitting at over 20 million views. (iDubbbzTV, n.d.)

Trouble in Paradise

Starting in 2016, Washburn began dating Anisa Jomha. She was also an online creator that streamed video games and made vlog style videos discussing dating, relationships, and being a female in a male dominated space (the gaming genre being dominated by men). By 2019, they appeared in each other's content. But they mainly kept their content separate. It was publicly known Jomha was Washburn's girlfriend.

On March 9, 2020, Jomha announced she would be starting an OnlyFans account. (KYM, 2020) OnlyFans is a direct creator support website, like Patreon, where the audience can directly contribute to a creator in exchange for perks and exclusive access. OnlyFans is dominated by amateur pornographic content. And Jomha did create content on OnlyFans which could be classified as softcore pornography - mainly lewd and topless photos.

This created a firestorm of controversy and criticism against Washburn and Jomha. In an effort to stay objective, let's ask a question: Why would someone do porn? I can think of three reasons. The first would be financial. You can make money doing it. The second would be sexual gratification. If you're an exhibitionist, exposing yourself to people provides self-satisfaction. And the last reason is attention seeking and validation. The ethics/morality around manufacturing adult content is beyond this book.

Many of these reasons became the starting point for the criticism and trolling they began to receive. Trolls made fun of the idea Jomha was broke and had a failing career, and she did it out of desperation. Many criticized why Washburn, such a successful creator, did not support Jomha financially, implying he would rather hold onto his money than support his girlfriend. Others criticized Jomha as a degenerate. But the most impactful criticism and what became the source of lots of trolling was the idea that Washburn was a cuckold, "simp", or he couldn't satisfy Jomha. Or Jomha was looking for other men. Trolls also teased Washburn with monikers like "Content Cuck", a play of his Content Cop character.

Early in the book we discussed how to deal with controversy: addressing, deflection, or silence. Washburn chose to address the controversy and attempted to downplay the whole thing. He responded to criticism in a video titled: "sex workers - idubbbz complains", released on March 28, 2020. I believe the original title was, "I'm OK With My Girlfriend Starting an OnlyFans". (iDubbbzTV, 2020) In the video, Washburn responded to the controversy by using humor. He said he was okay with his girlfriend doing OnlyFans. It is surprisingly well mannered compared to his early work.

While tempered in his words and language, there were problems for Washburn in his response - he waited way too long to give his response, he morally castigated those mocking him, and he never actually defended Jomha's decision to start an OnlyFans.

The first issue with his response was Washburn waited two weeks to respond to the controversy, which is an eternity in internet time. The story had time to circulate, and anyone in his audience, familiar with his work, and other creators who collaborated with him had heard about the story by the time he responded to it. If you are going to address it, it has to be done right away. In my opinion, the correct action (if you decided to respond at all) was to make a very short video or even just a tweet addressing the controversy within a day or so of the story blowing up. He completely lost control of the narrative by waiting that long.

The second issue was the response itself. Throughout the video the arguments he uses are not logical arguments. He starts out the video by saying he is cool with people making pornography. He goes on to say, "A good amount of people are just doing the reasonable thing and just making jokes and laughing about it. But there's a whole other group of people that feel personally devastated and betrayed. 'You lied to us!' First of all, I'm not your f**ing dad. If you don't want to look up to me anymore. That's fine. I don't want you to look up to me." He responded to the people making fun of him, with what he thought were logical arguments to refute them, for the following nine minutes of the video.

Near the end of the video he states, "I think what I've learned from this experience is that when you're speaking to a large group of people and, uh, there's some dudes in back shouting out their opinions like, 'I f**king hate thots. I hate wh***s. Women who sell their bodies online f**king suck. That's the worst.' Instead of ignoring that and just moving on with my lecture. It might be a better idea to point out those people and say, 'Yeah, I actually don't agree with that sh**ty opinion, um, because it seems like me just ignoring it has led to, like, a cultivation of a bunch of retards. That pretty much wraps up this video." He places some kind of responsibility on himself to "correct" people's behavior and opinions. He believes that by NOT responding, there will be people who are detractors. Therefore, by "correcting" the detractors he will have fewer detractors.

In the scenario he creates, an auditorium where he is essentially getting heckled, he sees it as his responsibility to stop his lecture, and whatever *he* wants to discuss, and refute the heckler. Here's the problem: You can't reason with unreasonable people. The only way to meet a heckler is to shout them down, have them removed, or what happens in stand-up comedy - the comedian starts mocking and making jokes at the heckler's expense. If you stop your public speaking and try to refute/debate/engage with the heckler, then everybody knows in order to get your attention, all they have to do is heckle you. People who heckle are disrupters. They aren't trying to engage in a good faith dialogue. It's like trolling, they are only there to get a reaction.

What Washburn did not realize with his approach is he rationalized reacting to detractors and trolls. That is the cardinal rule of the internet: don't feed the trolls. Now, as human beings we have weaknesses and sometimes people get under our skin and we react. But Washburn sees engaging with trolls as his *moral responsibility.*

The third issue with his video was that he never addresses the issue at hand: Why is Jomha doing it? Why is Washburn okay with her doing it? Jomha's name is not uttered once in the video. He doesn't rationalize or explain her decision. He also doesn't explain why he is okay with it. If his position was only to say, "I'm totally fine with it" which he does state near the end of the video, why not make the video one minute long? He didn't say, "Women's bodies should be free and beauty should be enjoyed". Or "I don't see sex work as degrading to women". Or "I support her decision". He couldn't even muster, "Her body, her choice. I love her no matter what". He doesn't address why people thought it was controversial.

The problem for Washburn was this would set the precedent once a controversy erupted, especially involving his partner, he would feel obligated to respond to it. Not just respond, but to engage in moral policing, just like his Content Cop character. Instead of going after public figures, he was going after random people in the comments section. *Content Cop* wasn't designed to reform or convince the target person, it was made for entertainment value. These response videos to trolls would also be done without any of the self-deprecating humor or comedy of a *Content Cop* video.

By June of 2020, Jomha stopped making OnlyFans content and uploaded a video titled: "Do I regret making an onlyfans?" (Jomha, 2020) In the video, she laments the extreme amount of criticism she faced, her body issues, and wanting financial independence. Near the end of the video, she states, "...it [the experience of doing an Onlyfans] just really helped me learn that there's no point in worrying about what/how people see you. The only thing that matters is you doing things that are important to you and being passionate about them and the people that don't like it will continue to not like it. And, and to be honest starting my OnlyFans was very empowering mentally and emotionally for me because those people I mean, I got, it was, it was a lot [of money] and it was fine. It was fine at the end of the day. Like, it didn't hurt me. You know. I'm here. I'm existing. I'm still doing very well on OnlyFans and just because these people are telling me they don't like it doesn't mean that I have to stop doing it. And, by me kind of ignoring, listening and ignoring those things has made me realize that I'm better off living the way that I want to live and just let people do what they want to do. And feel however they want to feel."

Jomha's response was, in my opinion, the better response. She refuses to give the haters power and dismisses the controversy.

This controversy made a large impact on the way people viewed Washburn, which is why we have covered it at length and as much context as possible was given. The overall feeling of Washburn's audience was very mixed to be generous but was mainly negative. Some didn't care and wanted him to continue making content. Others thought it was morally or ethically wrong. Or at least a betrayal of his original self. His balanced or lukewarm response contrasted heavily with his edgier past self. This also tested many of Washburn's friendships as he was on the receiving end of criticism, and many other creators distanced themselves from him. Others, like H3H3, defended both Washburn and Jomha.

Ian Washburn and Anisa Jomha did weather the controversy and continued the relationship. They eventually married in June of 2021. However, this marriage also created another controversy because Ian took his wife's last name. (Moving forward I will refer to them by their first names).

This sparked another round of mockery and trolling around the idea that Ian was a cuck, beta male, or simp. It also introduced the theory Anisa was the more dominant one in the relationship and did not respect Ian. It should be noted that Ian used a moniker: Ian Carter, before changing his name to Jomha. He was already not using his legal name as a public figure before his marriage.

Creator Clash 1 & 2

In January of 2022, Ian announced his next project: Creator Clash. Creator Clash was an influencer boxing event that would feature popular YouTube creators. The proceeds of this event would go to charity and Ian would also be fighting in this event. Having never boxed before, he began training at the Bonafide Boxing gym, in Seattle, under Michael Briggs. Per the gym's website, Michael Briggs has over 20 years of experience in martial arts and is, "passionate about coaching both pro and amateur fighters to reach their full potential." (Bonafide Boxing, n.d.)

Ian's regular content slowed throughout 2022. And understandably so. He was dedicated to training for the boxing event. Anisa took over organizing the event. Because Ian and Anisa were very well known and popular, this unlocked massive collaborative potential. They were able to convince other popular YouTube creators to join the event. Each would bring their audience's attention to the event and create cross pollination. Even creators who were not fighting were interested due to the charity aspect and networking opportunity. Ian and Anisa went on multiple different channels to discuss the event, including the H3 Podcast. H3H3, who had moved away from commentary content and moved into the podcasting space, promoted the event to his millions of listeners.

The event took place on May 14, 2022 and featured nine fights and 18 creators. The Yuengling Center in Tampa, FL had almost full attendance. There was also a Pay-Per-View. Ian did fight as the main event, but lost by decision. However, the event overall was a success. Ian announced in his video, "How I feel about my loss...", that the event raised over a million dollars for different charities. (iDubbbzTV, 2022) The event also created lots of positive attention for Ian and Anisa and they began to rehabilitate their image after the OnlyFans controversy.

Ian's time away from his YouTube channel did impact his content. He only posted two videos, not related to boxing, in 2022. Both did under one million views in 2022. But Ian seemed to be transitioning into boxing, and on January 23, 2023 he announced the sequel: Creator Clash 2.

Creator Clash 2 was facing a bit of a headwind compared to Creator Clash 1. CC1 was helped by the fact there were no large in person events that could be held because of Covid-19. Covid-19 shut down most in-person events through 2020 and 2021. Throughout 2022, in all sectors of the economy, in-person events were very popular due to pent up demand. By 2023, the world had mostly returned to normal. Originally, Ian was not going to be fighting in this event, sticking to promoting and managing. Ian was one of the largest creators in the first Creator Clash, so pulling him out of fighting was a loss.

The event initially was met with pushback over the selection of fighters. Many thought most of the fighters were no longer "relevant". They were 2010s YouTubers, this was the 2020s. They had peaked 5 years previously - an eternity in internet time. Many younger people didn't even know who they were.

Additionally, the novelty of the event had worn off. Influencers and YouTubers had already been boxing for several years. The very concept had been called into question. The first issue was not many creators are interested in boxing or the physical toll of boxing - so finding participants was difficult. Secondly, creators who participate in boxing have to step away from content creation to train. Stepping away from their core business is very expensive for creators. Thirdly, the audience wasn't interested in boxing. The "fun" wasn't watching boxing; these were amateur style fights. They were interested in the creator. The "sport" is just an excuse to get creators collaborating in person and have some competition.

Creator Clash 2 also ran into controversy. Froggy Fresh, a creator who was a fighter in the event, was taken off the fight card on March 26, 2023. At the time, no reason was given. It was speculated he was dismissed because Froggy had started training for the fight with Sam Hyde. Hyde was a creator who had experience with boxing. Hyde had trolled Ian in the past and made disparaging remarks towards Anisa. Ian disliked Hyde so much, he banned Hyde from Creator Clash 1.

Ian eventually responded to the controversy on his main channel in a 26-minute video titled: "Addressing the Froggy Fresh Drama" on May 3, 2023, (iDubbbzTV, 2023) almost a month and a half later. In the video, he admits it was a late response but did not want to jeopardize the event by discussing this controversy until after the fight. He further elaborates it would have been selfish to do it at the time. In my opinion, this was a good idea if you were going to get rid of someone. Drop them and remain silent. There were bigger fish to fry than this one creator. Simply removing him and moving on, and not spending any effort addressing, was the right thing to do. However, why make the video at this point? By this time, Creator Clash 2 had already happened. The controversy had been forgotten about. I'm not sure why Ian felt the need to go back and relitigate the entire controversy.

In this video, just as we saw with his "I'm OK With My Girlfriend Starting an OnlyFans"/"sex workers - idubbbz complains" the same pattern emerges: 1) he waited way too long to give his response, 2) he morally castigated his critics, and 3) he never really addresses the issue. The issue being: removing a popular creator for petty personal reasons from a charity boxing event when the event was struggling. Ian feels like it's his responsibility to respond to the trolls and correct the record. In the video, Ian begins to criticize and morally castigate both Hyde and Froggy. Both Froggy and Hyde had made negative comments towards Ian and Anisa. However, because Ian responded (being a larger channel), he unintentionally signal boosted those negative comments.

The problem with kicking Froggy Fresh off the card goes back to the very structure of influencer boxing: the audience is there for the influencer, not the sport. Froggy's fans, upon hearing the news he was removed, boycotted the event and began to criticize the event online. All the other Ian and Anisa detractors, looking for an opening to attack, also criticized the event. However, Ian and Anisa still had their own supporters and friends, like H3H3, who defended and promoted the event.

The event happened on April 15, 2023 and would end up losing money. Additionally, because the event needed a boost, Ian had to headline the event. He also lost his fight in a majority decision. In a video titled "The Harsh Reality of Creator Clash 2" Ian admitted the event lost $250,000.

(iDubbbzTV, 2023) Because of that, he would do additional streaming to try and recover the money. He admitted he thought CC2 would be larger and more successful than CC1. However, ticket sales and PPV buys were down - about half of CC1.

The failure of the event became a controversy in and of itself. Most of Ian and Anisa's detractors mocked, trolled, but also criticized their failure. They cited fighter mismanagement, event mismanagement, and overspending on accommodations and perks for the guests as reasons for the failure. Anisa, being the event planner, faced additional criticism. The financial mismanagement was so bad, many did not believe the event could lose so much money. Auditors from the event's financial backers investigated for embezzlement. Those embezzlement claims were false, it was just not managed well.

Macbeth and Lady Macbeth

In the Shakespearean tragedy *Macbeth*, Macbeth is a Scottish general who desires to take the throne from the King of Scotland. He is urged to murder the king by his wife, Lady Macbeth, and seize the throne. He does commit the murder and becomes King of Scotland. However, Macbeth becomes a tyrant. And both are driven to madness by guilt over their crimes.

Ian's usage of edgy humor, offensive language, and "bullying" other creators resulted in him becoming the "King of Scotland". It's how he was able to build his YouTube channel. It's how he built his brand. It's what made him relevant and famous. And while Ian was saying edgy jokes and went up to Tana Mongeau with the "Say N****r!" *Content Cop* - Anisa was right there with him. She later revealed publicly that she was the camera operator for that episode.

Ian and Anisa, Macbeth and Lady Macbeth, seem consumed with guilt over their past content and behavior. In my opinion, Ian wants the audience to share the guilt as well. Just as he profited off of Tana Mongeau's misfortune, the audience profited by laughing and being entertained. The guilt they feel over their past content has driven them mad. This madness had disastrous results for their career trajectory.

After Creator Clash 2, Ian returned to content creation on his main YouTube channel. He released a video on May 18, 2023, entitled: "I miss the old idubbbz". (iDubbbzTV, 2023) In the video, he addressed his critics who missed and were fond of the "edgier" content. He apologized for the content he made in the past and described it as hurtful, awful, and bigoted. This video fits the pattern: 1) he waited way too long to give his response, 2) he morally castigated his critics, and 3) he never really addresses the issue.

Ian referenced the Tana incident in his video. By this time, that was six years ago. He already moved onto other content. He morally disclaimed the content and said he was responsible for the audience's toxicity. The *actual issue* was his audience was frustrated with his boring content or even lack thereof, it wasn't he was making new or different content.

In the video, he claimed he felt he was bigoted in the past and those past videos don't represent him anymore. Ian goes on to state that he is ashamed to have learned empathy at the age of 32. "I've realized it because I just, like, can't help myself but, uh, like feel for other people's pain and suffering now. I'm still not perfect." He continues to end the video, "You can unlock ability empathy if you, you know, experience more life. It might take you getting hurt a little bit. But it's worth it. It is so worth it."

In my opinion, it was not *empathy* Ian was learning but rather *guilt*. This guilt constantly interferes with his decision-making process.

Earlier in the book, we discussed persona and the role it played in the creator's successful public image. Ian's persona was an edgy, irreverent, truth-telling comedian. Many of his jokes and humor nowadays might be considered going too far. His fanbase was full of people who liked this kind of humor. At this point, he was shifting away from that content, those fans, and changing his public persona. Many of those earlier fans were upset by his video because it made them feel like they were somehow morally or ethically wrong for enjoying past his content.

Ian went back to making content on his main channel. By this point, his content was seen as stale and he wasn't getting the same views that he had enjoyed previously. Some videos he released didn't even break 250,000 views. In the past, he could easily break over a million views.

Ian and Anisa started their own podcast on October 2, 2023, on a different channel called Maximum Damage. The podcast was named: *She Ruined My Career*. This was supposed to be an ironic reference to the meme circulating around Anisa being a "Yoko Ono character" who destroyed Ian's career. They also started doing a Spotify-exclusive podcast called *The Bog,* which was a paid podcast.

I was not able to locate viewership numbers on *The Bog. She Ruined My Career* was not successful. Many episodes of the podcast struggled to get 10,000 views. They review old movies, discuss current events or other internet drama, and many times they are simply making idle conversation. Commenters derided the podcast for being low-effort, low-energy, and boring.

These long form content videos also served as cannon fodder for trolls and detractors. Keeping with the lolcow tradition of oversharing, Ian and Anisa shared many personal stories. Many of these personal stories were compromising and embarrassing. Anisa told embarrassing stories about Ian, like his Irritable Bowel Syndrome, and how he occasionally soils himself. Ian has to sit down to pee because he has anxiety about public restrooms. Many episodes seem tense as they both *sneak diss* each other.

Creator Clash 3 & Israel v Palestine

It's difficult to explain how these seemingly unrelated events became intertwined with each other. Ian and Anisa were friendly with two other creators: Hasan Piker aka HasanAbi and Ethan & Hila Klein aka H3H3. Both did a podcast together called *Leftovers* which covered politics, pop culture, and other current events.

The Israeli-Gaza war began on October 7, 2023. Piker is hyper supportive of the Palestinian cause. He defended the October 7 attacks as justifiable military resistance. He went so far as to claim all Israeli settlers on Palestinian land were "occupiers" and were valid military targets, including children.

Piker was a fervent advocate for Palestine, almost too fervent. Because Klein was Jewish and his wife, is an Israeli Jew and former Israeli Defense Force conscript, they became the victim of many antisemitic comments. Ethan and Hila Klein have been critical of Israel's actions during the war. Ethan went so far as to refer to the ongoing war as a genocide against Palestinians. However, this was not enough to subvert the angry mob.

This caused an obvious rift between Piker and Klein. especially after Piker refused to condemn the antisemitic attacks on Ethan. The whole affair was its own controversy online and Piker and Klein ceased doing *Leftovers* after October 12, 2023. (H3 Podcast, 2023) And it was put on permanent hiatus on November 28, 2023. However, both Klein and Piker would continue to spar with each other over this issue.

Creator Clash 3 was announced on the Creator Clash channel on February 4, 2025 and on Ian's main channel on February 7, 2025. (iDubbbzTV, 2025) In the video, Ian explains what he thinks makes influencer boxing interesting: the element of "mystery". Who is going to train or not train? Who is going to win? And how does their background affect the fights? Ian also addresses his promise to make a documentary about Creator Clash 1, which he never delivered on. (See Lolcow Trait #4 - Failure to Deliver Promises) Ian acknowledges the failure of the last event and agrees to do more promotion (we'll come back to that).

Right out of the gate, Creator Clash 3 was facing an even larger head wind compared to CC1 and CC2. The general reaction was genuine criticism and trolling. Commenters thought the influencer boxer wave was over, many of the fighters were old and past their prime, and it wasn't clear how this event wasn't going to repeat the same mistakes of CC2.

Ethan and Hila Klein would continue to be targeted with antisemitic attacks, despite being critical of Israel's treatment of Palestinians. This included attacks made by rabid antisemite, BadEmpanada. The Kleins were sent human skulls to their house, which they interpreted as a death threat and called the authorities. This happened sometime in March 2025, but they did not publicly disclose that until April 2025.

These antisemitic attacks reached a climax on March 3, 2025 when Child Protective Services were sent to the Klein's home. Ethan announced Child Protective Services had been called on him on March 7, 2025 on their podcast. (H3 Podcast, 2025) What was the basis for this? Months prior, Ethan told a humorous story about his family members getting sick with giardia.

This story was pounced on by BadEmpanada. He is a creator who has devoted his channel to debunking Zionism, criticizing Israel, but also antisemitic attacks and rans about "Jewish conspiracies". He had also made many videos attacking Ethan and Hila Klein, including videos where he claims Hila (being an IDF conscript) is a terrorist and complicit in war crimes. (She was a secretary in an IDF office). BadEmpanada is so deranged that even Piker (a fervent Palestinian supporter) distanced himself from him (previously). You get the idea, he's a kook.

BadEmpanada began circulating statements that the Kleins were abusing their children. According to him, the Kleins refuse to clean up after their dogs and dog feces is all over their house. This dog feces was then eaten by their children, making them sick. BadEmpanada being a kook, with a very small channel, was then signal boosted by Piker's community - called the *Hasan orbiters*. These orbiters are also strong supporters of the Palestinian cause. One of these creators, DenimsTV, signal boosted these baseless accusations of child abuse. The comments section of DenimsTV streams were filled with people calling for CPS to be called. It is still unknown who called CPS - it was anonymous.

The CPS investigation was a formality, the truth is that the Kleins live in a decent home and their children are well taken care of.

How do Creator Clash 3, Anisa and Ian, and H3H3 intersect? Ian and Anisa were close with both the Kleins AND the Hasan orbiters. Denims aka Alexandra Saber, of DenimsTV, the creator who signal boosted BadEmpanada's rumor without challenging it and presented it as fact, is very close with Anisa.

In the March 7, 2025 video, where the Kleins announced CPS had been called on them, they referenced Ian and Anisa. It's not specifically stated when, but it's implied that immediately following the CPS call (March 3), but before the Kleins publicly acknowledged it (March 7), they reached out to Ian and Anisa. Would Anisa be okay with Denims spreading these heinous rumors against them? Would they make a public statement of support denouncing the false acquisitions? Would they come to the Klein's defense? Especially since Ian and Anisa had been to the Klein's house and would be in a unique position to defend them or debunk the slander. The Kleins requested Ian and Anisa publicly denounce these rumors: that they abuse their children or have dog feces all over their house.

Ian and Anisa chose to remain silent and did not make public statements to support the Kleins. In their March 7 video, the Kleins essentially declared them persona non grata. They expressed their frustration at their lack of support. They referenced their defense of Ian and Anisa through the OnlyFans controversy. Hila declared, "Thanks Anisa for standing up for your girl [sarcastic]. I actually stood up for you so many times 'cause like why, why would I not. It was crazy. People were sh**ting on you and Ian because you did OnlyFans, of course I was going to stand by you [as your friend]. That's insane. [that I wouldn't stand by you] It's absolutely insane and disgusting. But now you choose to hang out with people that would have a problem with you if you defended me. So, if you want to hang out with those people and have no spine and not stand up for another girl that stood up for you - enjoy your new friends." (H3 Podcast, 2025)

Ethan continued, "I just don't see how you can be my friend and also be friends with someone [Denims] like that." Hila replied later, "Well you can't. So, I already forgot about you [Anisa]." Hila later went on to say to Anisa, "Go f**k yourself."

Ethan and Hila felt very betrayed by Ian and Anisa. The whole stream was 3 hours long, but the betrayal was *so strong* they immediately addressed the Jomhas.

Remember Creator Clash 3, the charity boxing event that is supposed to be happening?.Well, it was still going on in the background or trying to get underway. But just like the section of this chapter, this whole Piker vs Klein controversy dominated. It was like a huge cloud hanging over the event. Fighters were training and event planning was already underway.

Ian and Anisa fell under immense scrutiny from the H3H3 community and from other detractors and trolls. It was almost unanimous: defending friends from clearly false and malicious rumors was the correct course of action. And business-wise, backing H3H3 was the correct move because they had a massive audience and had been strong supporters of the last two events. Or at the very least, assured the Kleins in private they were standing with them, but due to their precarious position in running a charity event weren't able to comment publicly on YouTube drama. However, the Jomhas were unable to navigate a middle ground and sided with Piker's camp.

Macbeth Attacks Macduff

In the play *Macbeth,* there is another Scottish lord, Macduff. After Macbeth has murdered the king, and becomes king, he throws a banquet. At this banquet, Macbeth invites all his Lords and Lady Macbeth to a night of drinking and merriment. However, Macduff refuses to attend. Macduff has left Scotland and gone to England to seek support to overthrow Macbeth. Macbeth orders Macduff's castle seized and sends assassins to kill everyone, including Macduff's wife and young son.

Ian, our Macbeth who used the n-word to seize the throne and now driven mad by guilt, is confronted with the Kleins' dissent against him. Klein is our Macduff. Let's recall back to Creator Clash 2 and Ian's delayed response to Froggy Fresh. In that video, Ian stated that he waited so long to address the controversy because he didn't want to jeopardize the event. However, this time, Ian would seek out to destroy the Kleins.

On April 16, 2025, Ian released "Content Cop – H3H3". (iDubbbzTV, 2025) Ian hadn't made a *Content Cop* in fix years. He dragged the character out of retirement to launch a strike against former his friend, Ethan Klein. The video was one hour and six minutes long, which was long by *Content Cop* video standards. It got millions of views. The video itself was a lengthy seethe session against Ethan by Ian. Ian attacked Ethan for attacking Ian's friend: Denims.

The whole video made no mention of the CPS call, which was crucial context in this spat. Ian was essentially saying Ethan and Hila were attacking people, he was friends with, but he never provided the reason why Ethan and Hila were upset with the people they were attacking. Ian's recall of events doesn't match the timeline.

As I understand it:

1. Israel vs Palestine war happens
2. H3H3 is on the receiving end of antisemitism because they are Jewish (despite being very critical of Israel)
3. An antisemitic kook begins baseless rumors that the Kleins abuse their kids
4. These rumors get signal boosted by Hasan orbiters, including Denims. The Jomhas are friends with Denims.
5. The Kleins have CPS called to their house, based on these false accusations
6. The Kleins reach out to Ian and Anisa for a public statement of support and are ignored.
7. The Kleins go on their podcast and denounce Denims, Anisa, Ian, and others

The way that Ian tells the story in his Content Cop on H3:

1. The Kleins reach out to Ian and Anisa for a public statement of support and are ignored.
2. The Kleins go on their podcast and denounce Demins, Anisa, Ian, and others
3. Ian, by making the Content Cop, is defending himself and his friends.

As you can see, Ian doesn't provide the full context. Which is why if you know the history and watch his *Content Cop* on H3H3 you can easily become confused. What is the criticism Ian has for Ethan? I'm not really sure. In my opinion, Ian's criticism amounts to moral grandstanding, personal attacks on Ethan, and bitterness towards Ethan. The video opens with Ian, at Hasan Piker's house, joined by Hasan orbiters: Denims, Frogan, and SeanDaBlack. They are Fortnite dancing and repeat, "Wake Up Ethan" as some kind of gotcha moment. Later on, Ian and Anisa would post a photo flipping off the camera directed at H3H3. There would also be a photo of Ian, taken at Piker's house, wearing a Palestinian flag and holding a sword with a swastika on the hilt. Some interpreted Ian's actions as an antisemitic dog whistle, since the Kleins are Jewish and had just been sent human skulls in the mail.

Macduff Attacks Macbeth and Lady Macbeth

In the play *Macbeth*, upon hearing the news of Macbeth's attack on his family, Macduff is stricken with grief but soon turns to vengeance against Macbeth. He rallies an army and goes back to Scotland to retake the throne.

H3H3 reacted to Ian's video in a full podcast, on April 16, 2025. (H3 Podcast, 2025) On the regular h3h3Productions channel, he posted a more succinct video that was 16 minutes long on April 20, 2025. (h3h3Productions, 2025) Ethan states in the video, "Ian spends the majority of his video characterizing me like a raving lunatic who's lashing out at everyone around me with zero provocation." and continues to say, "he doesn't explain why I'm upset, who I'm mad at, why I'm mad at them. Zero context." Ethan also points out that Ian never mentioned the CPS call in his *Content Cop*.

Ethan thought this attack on his family was an extreme provocation, line-crossing, and despicable event. His friends, the Jomhas, refused to defend him and his family. And not only did they fail to help him in his time of need, but they attacked *him* for responding to being attacked.

H3H3 has become the largest detractor channel against Ian and Anisa. He constantly criticizes, mocks, and trolls the Jomhas. H3H3 signal-boosts every negative story about them. He provides a massive platform for others to come and criticize them, even stating he will never stop attacking Ian.

Remember Creator Clash 3? I hope you haven't forgotten. Just like this section of the book, everyone else forgot about it as well. So much negative attention was on Ian and Anisa at this point, support for the event disintegrated. The majority of creators rallied behind the Kleins and against Ian. Fighters who were in the middle of training were beset by controversy and didn't know how to respond. The official Creator Clash organization wasn't communicating with its fighters. Speculation online swirled if the event would even happen.

This speculation turned out to be correct. As the toxicity around Ian and Anisa went supercritical, fighters began to drop out of the event throughout April 2025 - Harley Morenstein (the headliner), Lena Ayad (an associate of H3H3), LA Beast, and Myth. To try and stop the bleeding, the official Creator Clash Twitter on May 3, 2025, announced Ian and Anisa would be stepping down from Creator Clash. By July 7, 2025, the event would be officially cancelled.

Macbeth's Rule Comes to an End

As Macduff besieges Macbeth's castle, Macbeth delivers the most famous soliloquy of the play:

> Tomorrow, and tomorrow, and tomorrow
> Creeps in this petty pace from day to day
> To the last syllable of recorded time;
> And all our yesterdays have lighted fools
> The way to dusty death. Out, out, brief candle!
> Life's but a walking shadow, a poor player

That struts and frets his hour upon the stage
And then is heard no more. It is a tale
Told by an idiot, full of sound and fury
Signifying nothing.

Macduff and his forces storm the castle. Macduff meets Macbeth in a duel. Macbeth is killed offstage. Macduff re-enters with Macbeth's severed head. He then invites all to see himself be crowned king.

Ethan Klein became the lightning rod for everyone who had been burned by the Jomhas. Harley Morenstein and Nathan Barnatt aka Dad, two creators who were fighters in CC3, both appeared on his show to air grievances and express displeasure at the whole affair.

Klein was able to secure a bombshell interview with Michael Briggs and his wife, Kate Briggs, on June 4, 2025. (H3 Podcast, 2025) Briggs was the boxing coach who trained Ian for CC1 and CC2. They both had spent extensive time with the Jomhas. They told numerous and embarrassing stories and confirmed many rumors and speculations.

They said Anisa regularly emasculated Ian. For example, she smiled when she saw him get beaten up in sparring practice. Anisa had a crush on another fighter at the gym. Anisa told them she had done pornography. Ian smelled bad and didn't shower in-between training sessions. Ian was very sensitive and when Michael scolded Ian, he started to cry because Michael reminded him of his father. Anisa also broke down in tears after someone else in the gym mocked the music she started playing. Additionally, while Michael tried to comfort Anisa and apologize, Ian was aloof and didn't care to support his wife. Ian was also lazy and didn't keep up with his training regimen.

Both Briggs also expressed displeasure with the Jomhas overall attitude and personality. They felt the Jomhas were conceited, self-centered, difficult to deal with, and unappreciative. Also, had refused to pay a bonus. The Briggs also noted they were not invited to the post-Creator Clash party, while everyone else was, despite him being Ian's coach. Also, Kate requested they voice support for legislation she was lobbying for. She has been working to ban child marriage. (Child marriage is somehow still legal in some states.) Because they were public figures with a wide reach, it could help the cause. Anisa ghosted her and refused to respond. But once Anisa learned they would be on the *H3 Podcast* as a guest, she quickly reached out in a vain attempt to get them not to go on.

Overall, the internet erupted in a unanimous disgust at the Jomhas. Ian tried to respond to the accusations in a video titled: "Coming clean..." on September 9, 2025. (iDubbbzTV, 2025) But again, this video suffered the same Ian pattern: 1) he waited way too long to give his response (3 months had passed already), 2) he morally castigated his critics, and 3) he never really addresses the issue. But by this time, everyone had already made up their minds. Ian and Anisa were universally disliked.

The Aftermath

Anisa no longer makes content on her own channel. She returned to OnlyFans on August 20, 2025. She occasionally posts on social media - mainly about current events, cooking, and her dogs.

Ian has moved onto Twitch and has long streams while playing video games. He has copied the style of Hasan Piker's lengthy Twitch streams, but much more lackluster. His streams average between 150 to 350 viewers, which is considered low. Trolls and detractors watch his content to see him clumsily dance, ramble, and mock him. He continues to try and explain himself and morally police the comments section.

Ian Jomha did not respond to a request for comment.
Anisa Jomha did not respond to a request for comment.

Troll names:
Content Cuck
Simple Ian
The NF Guy - referencing his past usage for the n-word and f-slur

You can use this QR Code to go to Idubbbz's main YouTube channel:

161

Chapter 11: Jeremy Hambly aka TheQuartering

Jeremy Hambly aka TheQuartering is relatively new to the lolcow arena. It is even debatable whether he is a lolcow at all. He grew to prominence making videos criticizing the politicization of popular culture. That quickly turned into a constantly expanding enterprise with diminishing returns.

Jeremy Hambly was born in April of 1983 and lives in Wisconsin. He is a content creator that wears many hats. Hambly covers a variety of topics. Everything from claw machines, RC cars, Magic: The Gathering, to politics and news. He has so many YouTube channels it's hard to catalogue them all. It's also possible there are others that have been lost to time. He is most well-known as: TheQuartering.

Hambly's personal life is closely guarded. Of all the people we discuss in this book, he is by far the most capable of keeping his private life separate. However, as we will read later in the chapter, there are times he slips up. It is known Hambly married his high school sweetheart. While we don't know exactly where Hambly worked before becoming a YouTuber, he did allude to it earlier in his career.

Hambly gave an interview with Eric Hunley on December 9, 2021. Eric Hunley runs a YouTube channel discussing human behavior. (Eric Hunley, 2021) In the interview, Hambly described his early life. He started working in a computer store around the age of 17 until 20 and handled computer repairs.

He stated that he started making "tutorial" videos on YouTuband he has been on YouTube for twenty years or pretty close to that amount. He started his first business creating "home repair kits" for computers and he sold that to an internet company. He then started a different YouTube channel.

He also stated he started making websites for businesses in the early 2000s as his own business. Around this time, there was a wave of businesses getting connected to the internet. Many people were less familiar with technology and many web tools we have today did not exist yet.

At the time of the interview in 2021, he was still working in the corporate world for a marketing company. His specialization was CRO (conversation rate optimization) and click through rates for websites and e-commerce. He describes his job designing websites. For example, using certain colors and fonts which appeal to people psychologically to drive sales. It could be seen as subtle manipulation. He states in the video, "I don't use this on my viewers, but I use this at my day job."

It should be noted that Hambly started on YouTube while still working a day job, as he would allude to in earlier videos. I do remember him, (and I can't find the exact video) stating that due to the volatility of YouTube, leaving your day job wasn't the correct career move for most people as YouTube careers are short.

Hambly's background in marketing will explain the sheer amount of content he creates and his "working" the algorithm for clicks and views. The story of Hambly begins with him exploring his passions, but ends in the hamster wheel of grinding out content.

The Content Factory

Hambly has had so many channels over the years that I felt it was necessary to create a chart to help visualize. The sheer amount of content and varying topics is unique. Just like his "TheQuartering" moniker, he seems to split up elements of his person across different channels.

Channel	Subscribers as of Sept 2025	Active Uploads	Genre
rcnightmare	64,000	Aug 2010 to Present	RC cars
Unsleeved Media	142,000	Feb 2012 to Oct 2022	Magic the Gathering
ClawStruck	108,000	Nov 2014 to April 2020	Claw machines
Midwestly	Now deleted	Oct 2019 to Feb 2022	politics
TheQuartering	1,900,000	Jul 2017 to Present	politics/pop culture
Exclusively Games	33,000	Dec 2018 to Jun 2020	Video games
Jeremy Hambly	164,000	April 2024 to Oct 2025	Personal channel
Community Notes	23,000	Feb 2023 to Aug 2023	politics
ThePublica	18,000	April 2023 to Sept 2024	politics
Quartering Live	326,000	July 2025 to Present	politics/pop culture

The first channel that I could find he uploaded to is rcnightmare, a channel focusing on remote-controlled vehicles. These are not just toys for children, they can cost thousands of dollars per vehicle. This seems to be an early passion project for Hambly. He still uploads to the channel, although not regularly. What is interesting is that he doesn't link this channel or promote it at all.

The second channel Hambly started was Unsleeved Media. It was devoted to another passion of Hambly's, *Magic: The Gathering*. Magic, or MTG as it's known, is a strategy game that uses collectible cards. Early videos were unboxing videos, discussing strategy, and reviews. He also discussed what was happening in the overall MTG community and Wizards of the Coast, the maker of the game. Hambly became increasingly critical of Wizards of the Coast over what he described as politicization of the game's community.

Unsleeved Media was a very prolific channel and has over 1,500 videos. Hambly states his increasing criticism against Wizards of the Coast and members of the MTG community pushing progressive politics got him banned for life from MTG events on December 7, 2017. The official reason for the ban was threats he made at Grand Prix Las Vegas - which is a MTG live event. Hambly disputes the reason for his ban. (Hipsters Staff, 2017)

Hambly continued to make videos on Unsleeved Media, but this time used his platform to speak negatively about MTG events. In a November 26, 2018 video, he called on people to boycott the Grand Prix. (UnsleevedMedia, 2018)

Hambly started TheQuartering as an offshoot of his main channel, which at the time was Unsleeved Media. He calls it TheQuartering because, "everyone is pulling everyone in every other direction. And what I want to do is kind of like reassemble the human body here, metaphorically." (TheQuartering, 2017) In the first video still public, posted July 13, 2017, Hambly expresses his frustration on the intrusion of politics into the MTG community and the "affirmative action" selection process for MTG judges. He argued for a meritocratic system. He also describes himself as fiscally conservative, but liberal on every other issue.

His early videos were still about MTG but also started covering YouTube topics. In the beginning, his channel covered live events. For example, he went to Mythcon Milwaukee in September 2017 and covered it in a video he posted October 11, 2017. (TheQuartering, 2017) This was at the tail end of the popularity around the YouTube atheism/skeptic genre. YouTube Atheism was a genre that featured debates between fundamentalist Christians and atheists on YouTube. He also started covering news stories about other online content creators. TheQuartering mainly stuck to pop culture topics. Over time most of his videos complained about politics getting involved with something - a video game, movie franchise, actor, etc.

By February 16, 2018, TheQuartering had 38,000 subscribers, and regularly got 10,000 to 50,000 views per video. (TheQuartering, 2018) By this time, he was already consistently uploading two to three videos per day. He was interviewed by Milo Yiannopoulos, a conservative SJW critic, who was at the height of his popularity, about the SJW influence in the video game industry. He was treated as an expert on the subject.

The Culture War Grift

The term *grift* goes all the way back to the early 1900s and is slang for con artist or street hustler. *Online grifting* is not an illegal practice, but does use some of the same confidence man tactics. Online grifters use the internet to deceive, manipulate, or emotionally exploit people for money or influence, often under the guise of sincerity, activism, or entertainment. Common forms of online grifting are:

1. Charity & Crowdfunding
2. Lifestyle/Self-Help
3. Financial Advice
4. Drama
5. Ideological or Political

Charity and crowdfunding grifts are utilized by creators to extract money by manufacturing emergencies and requesting sympathy. Usually, the cause is exaggerated or fabricated. The funds are diverted to something else. For example, a creator may claim their pet is sick and crowdfund the vet bill, but the dog is fine. Or the vet bill wasn't as high as they portrayed to the audience.

Lifestyle/Self-Help grifts sell the illusion of success and if you give the grifter money, they can help you become successful too. Most of these grifters sell coaching or advice. This is usually common sense or readily available information. They also make false claims of success. The grifter is usually not successful using the techniques they sell. For example, a fitness guru who wants you to buy his workout course so you can look buff like him, except he secretly uses steroids.

Financial advice grifts are very similar to lifestyle grifts, but for personal finances. These grifters portray themselves as financially very wealthy and want to share the "secrets" of their success with you for a small fee. This is usually a course they sell, access to stock trades, or invitation to seminars. For example, they sell you a course on options trading, but it is usually recycled information.

Drama grifts use emotional manipulation to keep the audience tuning in and giving views. These views translate into more money, they rely on outrage to drive views. Drama grifters pick fights or feuds with other online creators. They may stretch out and exaggerate the drama. And, naturally, they frame themselves as the victim or persecuted - even if they start the drama. For example, a drama grifter might insult a far bigger channel over a nonissue hoping for a response. This response would then provide their channel with more attention.

This brings us to the last kind of grifter, Ideological or Political. These grifters turn ideology or identity into a monetized fandom. They use fear, outrage, or sympathy. They amplify culture-war issues to drive division. They use Us Vs Them framing. They frequently demonize the other side, and frame themselves as the victim, truth-teller, or martyr. They may use phrases like: "They are silencing me" or "They are trying to cancel me". They also shift opinions based on what is profitable, rather than being consistent.

By creating, fomenting, or plugging into outrage, they can sell themselves and products to this emotionally charged audience. They drive donations, merch sales, or subscriptions for some sort of struggle or political cause. As long as the audience supports them, they can continue to "fight" for them or whatever cause.

To be clear, these political grifters exist on every possible political spectrum. Everything from anarchists to communists. And on almost every political issue. There is a difference between political lobbying or activism, and grifting. Lobbyists and activists take real identifiable political action; grifters do not.

Around the late 2010s, many large companies began creating advertisements with left wing messaging, seen as corporate activism. Nike partnered with black activist Colin Kaepernick in September 2018. He was an NFL player who kneeled during the national anthem before games which became a national controversy. Even the CEO of BlackRock, in 2018, wrote about the need for "diversity" in their company as well as wanting to make sure other companies had diversity.

Gillette did an ad targeting "toxic masculinity" in January of 2019.

We should note for context, the changing political culture around this time. In the late 2000s, there was the collapse of the Reagan/Bush or neoconservative right wing due to the unpopularity of the Iraq War and 2008 financial crisis. This led to the 2008 election of Barack Obama, and the "rainbow coalition" he created. Throughout the 2010s. there was the rise of SJW activism, gaining lots of popularity in the Black Lives Matter movement of 2014-2015. This was then followed by the MAGA movement. During 2015 and into 2016, as Trump was elected, BLM and SJWs lost ground. By 2019, "woke" was being used as a pejorative term to mock the far-left policies and ideology of SJWs. By the early 2020s, "woke" was on the decline. By 2024, with the landslide election of Trump, the right now has the upper hand.

This brings us back to Hambly. Hambly originally expressed frustration with the encroachment of politics into aspects of life in his early TheQuartering videos. This was his bread and butter grift. He wasn't explicitly right wing or left wing. He was a politically neutral grift. He would gather an audience which was also upset at what he believes is an SJW or leftwing influence into gaming, popular culture, and other issues. He was upset about it, and the audience could join him and be upset about it too. (Because he only attacks one side, the left, you could categorize him as right.)

In 2018, TheQuartering had 38,000 subscribers. By 2020, Hambly had one million subscribers. It was a meteoric rise. There was clearly a market for his *grift.*

So, how does this culture war grift work? Let's take an example from Hambly's channel. Hambly has made a cottage industry out of making Brie Larson content. He has made over 91 videos about Larson or putting her in the thumbnail or title of the video. (I stopped counting after 91, so there may be more) Larson was the actress who played Captain Marvel in the Marvel cinematic universe. She is a well-known left-leaning actress who discusses feminism, anti-racism, etc. Regardless of her politics, she also does not enjoy a good reputation as far as working with other actors and can come across as preachy or out of touch.

What is the standard formula for a TheQuartering video? Let's take one of the 91 videos at random. This video was released on July 4, 2022, has over 100,000 views and is 11 minutes, 30 seconds long titled: "Brie Larson BLASTED By the Media!! Called a Friendless LOSER & Lame! Captain Marvel Star Blasted!" (TheQuartering, 2022)

1. He reads an article that paints Brie Larson in a bad light
2. He proceeds to dunk, mock, and ridicule Larson
3. Ends the video lamenting how bad Larson is.

This video slightly breaks from the formula because there is no ad read by Hambly either plugging his products or his website - most likely because it is an older video.

That sounds like a very simple formula – because it is. Another popular target is Jimmy Kimmel. He has over 50 videos (I stopped counting) on Kimmel. Some are seven years old. In September of 2025, he uploaded multiple. Let's take a random video on Kimmel: "Jimmy Kimmel Epstein DISASTER Gets Worse! Old Disgusting Comments Resurface & Go VIRAL!" It came out on January 5, 2024 and has over 240,000 views and is 12 minutes, 31 seconds long. (TheQuartering, 2024)

1. Ad read - this time plugging his Facebook page

2. He reads an article that paints Jimmy Kimmel in a bad light
3. He proceeds to dunk on, mock, and ridicule Kimmel for being "woke"
4. Ends the video lamenting how bad Kimmel is

This formula is repeated by Hambly regarding other celebrities, activists, Disney, Bud Light, Marvel, Star Wars, transgenders etc. Just whatever is trending, current events, or in the news as controversial. Anything that can be framed in a Right (good, winning, and popular) vs Left (bad, SJW or woke, unpopular) way he will make a grift video on.

Hambly seemed to have located the fabled *Infinite Money Glitch* - internet slang for a loophole or system you can exploit to generate endless money. He was milking the same unlikable figure or controversy repeatedly. For YouTubers like Hambly, he was creating content out of a constant outrage cycle.

The Video Game Grift

Hambly started Exclusively Games in February of 2019 as a response to what he saw as the leftist and SJW intrusion into video games. He was able to raise $130,000 with crowdfunding to start the site and YouTube channel. Hambly stated the goal was an apolitical video game review and news site. "Our vision is simple. Cover gaming, video games, board games, tabletop games, whatever it is that you like to get away from daily life and to do it completely apolitically, 100% ad free, and 100% in the service of the community." Twice a year they would reach out to request donations. They would also sell merchandise. Six months after launching the site, Hambly says they have over 50,000 subscribers. (Exclusively Games, 2019)

As Hambly explains in a video titled: "The Future of Exclusively Games" after hiring staff, expenses grew. The channel struggled to get enough views (5,000 to 10,000 views per episode) to pay the staff. And eventually the seed money he put into the company was used up, and with lack of revenue, he decided to move on from the project. This was announced on June 23, 2020. (Exclusively Games, 2020) Jeremy states in the video the channel failed due to not advertising it enough. He also states there was no market for the neutral content that the website produced.

I want you to keep that in mind, as this would become a recurring pattern: 1) Launching a new project whose only defining feature is being non-political, 2) expanding staff and growing expenses, 3) lack of market demand, and 4) the project losing money and having to close.

The Politics Grift

Midwestly was originally his politics channel, now deleted. In TheQuartering videos, it was usually a link in the description. I was able to find this channel linked in videos from October 2019 to February 2022. Hambly was still referencing this channel in 2022, so it may have been deleted at that time. I wasn't able to find a public statement by Hambly on the closure of Midwestly, but I speculate because he covered politics on his main channel, TheQuartering, Midwestly was redundant.

Hambly repeats the same culture war grift, but over political figures and issues.

Live Stream Grift

Hambly started a livestream called *Community Notes* with Sydney Watson in April of 2023. They discussed popular culture, current events, and politics. *Community Notes* ended after Watson wanted to focus on ThePublica.

Hambly started another livestream, *QuarteringLive*. It is hosted by himself, with co-hosts Melanic Mac and Hannah-Claire Brimlow. The show mainly covers culture topics, current events, and politics. Hambly reports it is not profitable. He constantly drives memberships and ads to recuperate the money it takes to operate. The expenses, as he reveals to the audience, are paying his cohosts $500 a show. Every show costs at least $1,000 to run, which is very expensive for a show that reports to get 10,000 to 30,000 live viewers. (Kino Casino Clips, 2025)

The News Grift

ThePublica was launched on April 17, 2023. In the announcement video, Hambley states the goal of ThePublica was, "There's still a need, I believe, for a truly transparent news source. Not one that's owned by a super huge mega corporation that has financial backers to worry about. Not one that's owned by stockholders. But one that's owned by the actual people who consume the news." (The Publica, 2023) ThePublica had at least five writers, multiple videographers, and its own website.

This website would make its own content like, "daily news articles", "op-eds", "long deep dive pieces", and five new podcasts available.

ThePublica's closure was announced on September 27, 2024, on TheQuartering. The YouTube channel and the website didn't get enough traffic to generate the ad revenue needed to pay everyone. (TheQuartering, 2024)

The top comments of that video remark:

- "I do not know how you could not have seen this coming. It's essentially an online newspaper. Newspapers, in all forms and formats, are a dying entity."
- "As other people stated, you should have pushed your media site like you do with your coffee."
- "Not gonna lie. Your coffee was mentioned alot. I've never heard of this other one. I know Sydney Watson though"
- "If you had pushed it 20% as hard as CBC it could've flourished"
- "I think I remember hearing about The Publica once between the thousands of coffee promotions."

Hambly folded ThePublica over into TheQuartering.com. Hambly later stated on livestream Watson talked poorly about him behind his back. And she reached out to other female creators and advised them not to work with him. Hambly goes on to say that he paid for everything with ThePublica and assisted her with starting her tea business (like his coffee business). He revealed he lost between $100,000 to $250,000 on ThePublica. (Kino Casino Clips, 2025)

The Coffee Grift

Coffee and politics are strangely connected in the United States. If you study American history, you've probably heard about the Boston Tea Party during the American Revolution. Americans who were fed up with tea taxes dumped tea into Boston harbor. Americans refused to pay the tax and started drinking coffee, which was seen as patriotic.

According to the National Coffee Association, 66% of Americans drink coffee daily. (National Coffee Association of USA, Inc., 2025)

Hambly began promoting a coffee business called Coffee Brand Coffee in May of 2022. (Yes. That's its real name.) In a now deleted Facebook post announcing the opening, he states, "After years of sitting on the sidelines and watching powerlessly as everything from big budget Disney Movies to Ice Cream & Even Comic Books forced politics onto their customers in ways that at best divided them and at worst outright attacked them, I decided to do something about it." Many online conservative commentators sell their own coffee. In fact, selling coffee as merchandise is fairly common for YouTubers. It's like T-shirts, mugs, or fridge magnets. It's a way of supporting a creator while getting a small token.

However, Hambly promoted Coffee Brand Coffee as "non-political", most likely trying to make his coffee unlike the "leftwing" coffee like Starbucks, and the "rightwing" coffee sold by other conservative commentators.

As a product, how does Coffee Brand Coffee stack up compared to other coffee brands? There are varying degrees of roast (light to dark), extra caffeine, and multiple flavored coffees including butterscotch toffee, blackberry cream, blueberry cobbler, and strawberries n' cream. A 12 oz bag sells for $18 to $20. (Coffee Brand Coffee, 2025) It is a premium price for coffee.

It appears Hambly wants Coffee Brand Coffee to compete against the most premium coffee from artisan local roasters. The reviews for CBC (that's what I'll refer to moving forward) are good. But the price makes it unaffordable for everyday consumption for most people.

Hambly's promotion of CBC started in 2022 but really went into overdrive in 2023. He seemingly mentioned it in every video, much to the chagrin of his audience. He even references the fact that people hate the ads and his plugging the coffee is a "meme at this point", but then goes right into the ad. By 2024, his audience was turning against CBC. In the comments section of all his videos, viewers discuss their displeasure at the constant ads.

On March 20, 2025, in a video titled: "Woke Leftists Just SCREWED Me Over & All My Staff...", Hambly claims a vendor he worked with decided to stop doing business with him because of Hambly's politics - although he admits he can't prove that. (TheQuartering, 2025)

Hambly states he does not drop ship his coffee and hopes it will be on grocery store shelves. He says they are vertically integrated - everything from roasting the beans to printing the bags. Hambly says he is financially stressed, being $300,000 in debt over the coffee business. He is selling off his old video game systems to make ends meet, and he spent $80,000 to buy more equipment. He goes on to advertise his "Founders Vault Pack". He also wants to make a retail store. And he ends the video by requesting viewers buy the coffee to "stick it to this guy." A similar pattern to his politics/culture war grifts.

Hambly promotes CBC as a small American company which handles their own coffee production. Is this true? In 2022, internet detectives went to work through the CBC promotional material. The video of their "factory" looked suspiciously like Millcreek Coffee Roasters in Salt Lake City, UT. (BestOfTheBad TV, 2022) Millcreek Coffee Roasters does offer private label coffee. Lending credence to this theory is that the CBC company was incorporated on

April 4, 2022 in Utah. However, the company location in the LLC paperwork is in Wisconsin, where Hambly lives. The "physical address" listed is actually a virtual office in Milwaukee, WI owned by Davinci Virtual for $79 a month. (Davinci Virtual, 2025) Many businesses use a virtual office.

I went to the Wisconsin Department of Agriculture, Trade, and Consumer website. All food processors in Wisconsin must have a Food Processing Plant License. There is a list of all food companies in Wisconsin. I searched with the company name, variations of the company name, and Jeremy Hambly. In Wisconsin, there are 95 businesses which have the word "coffee" in the name, this is everything from a large factory to your local coffee shop. Coffee Brand Coffee is not listed.

I went to the CBC website. They don't have a mailing address or physical location listed anywhere. They don't have a phone number. (I was hoping I could locate it based on their phone number area code.) The only way of communicating with them was by email.

I reached out to Millcreek Coffee Roasters. They advised they are not able to provide any information on private label coffee.

I was not able to confirm *absolutely* that Coffee Brand Coffee is repackaged Millcreek Coffee Roasters. In an email to me, CBC stated their coffee is shipped out of Phoenix, AZ. I contacted Coffee Brand Coffee multiple times, requesting information on the origin of their coffee, where is their production facility, and if they would confirm or deny they are Millcreek Coffee Roasters private label coffee. They did not respond to those questions.

Work Less Smart, and More

"Work smarter, not harder" is a common saying, but not for Hambly. He seems to be intent on constant growth - new projects, new channels, and new products. The only successful project Hambly has is TheQuartering. It is his core business.

Midwestly, his political channel, was folded into TheQuartering. Exclusively Games failed, ThePublica failed, Coffee Brand Coffee is failing, and *QuarteringLive* is failing. This keeps with his pattern:

1. Launching an expensive new project whose only defining feature is being non-political
2. Expanding staff and growing expenses
3. Lack of market demand
4. The project losing money and having to close

Just as Hambly was expanding his businesses and projects, the core business, TheQuatering ,was declining.

Hambly uploads more videos now than he did in the past. TheQuartering used to upload three videos a day, back in 2020. It went up to four uploads a day sometime in 2022. As of 2025, he uploads five videos a day.

He also livestreams more than ever. In the past, livestreams were occasional occurrences. Usually, they were interviews or collaborations with other creators. He then made it a regular Sunday show starting in 2022. Now, it's a daily livestream. Hambly also started a daily stream on Rumble that airs 5 days a week which lasts for around 2 hours. These more frequent live streams started around July 2025. His regular TheQuartering videos are also uploaded on Rumble.

TheQuartering reached one million subscribers by December of 2020. (TheQuartering, 2020) Hambly reached 1.5 million subscribers on July 23, 2024, as he announced on his Twitter. By September of 2025, Hambly sits at 1.9 million subscribers. (Social Blade, 2025)

In September of 2020, The Quartering averaged 626,000 daily views and a weekly average of 4,387,320 views. According to Social Blade in September of 2025, TheQuartering is averaging 502,000 average daily views and 2,340,512 average weekly views. Despite TheQuartering having more subscribers than he had in 2020, and making more videos, it has approximately 125,000 fewer daily views and approximately 2,000,000 fewer weekly views.

How does that translate into money earned? We don't know how much TheQuartering earns. But we could approximate how much a channel could make using: Cost per 1,000 monetized views, or CPM. $2 per CPM is low, and $5 per CPM is high.

	Daily Views	$2 CPM - Yearly Revenue	$5 CPM Yearly Revenue
Sept 2020	625,000	$319,375	$798,438
Sept 2025	500,000	$255,500	$638,750

*assuming 70% monetization, not every video is monetized.

Assuming TheQuartering's numbers are similar to this, Hambly would still be making several hundred thousand dollars a year and be in the top 1% of YouTube channels. However, once you factor in all the failed projects that eat away at his income, the picture is less optimistic. He lost several hundred thousand dollars on ThePublica and Coffee Brand Coffee - he publicly stated this. Both of those projects could have destroyed an entire year's worth of profitability. We can safely say that he has entered his stagnation or decline phase. (TheQuartering, 2025)

Hambly's Spending

As Hambly's constant advertising about his products and urging his audience to "support" became featured more and more in his videos, people began a-logging (cataloguing) what he was spending money on.

Hambly's house, a mansion on 30 acres of land, is assessed at almost two million dollars, which is a lot for rural Wisconsin. People began to keep track of his Rolex watch collection as they would feature on his wrist in photos he posted online. He posted about his Tesla Cybertruck and hinted at other expensive vehicles he owns. He owns at least one plane. He also has a garage full of RC cars, each approximately $1,000 each, and a track for him to race his RC cars.

He posted on Twitter about his seven-foot tall saltwater aquarium in 2025. He hired someone part-time to manage it for him. (These fish later died due to tank mismanagement). He let small details slip on livestream, like wanting to build a greenhouse to grow citrus trees (he lives in Wisconsin). Many trolls/detractors mock him for his wasteful spending.

Hambly's Self-Defecating Humor

Many YouTubers struggle when going from short edited 10-minute videos to hours of long *unedited* live content. It is a different form of media. Podcasters and radio hosts make it look easy and spontaneous, but there is a lot of work and craft going into presenting and hosting a live multi-hour show. As Hambly began to do more long form content, he relaxed his position around sharing personal details with the audience and his hosts.

Because Hambly was live streaming frequently by 2022, and daily by 2025, he had to spend long hours on his computer. It turns out that Hambly has issues with bowel movements and frequently must step away. This came up as an issue as he began to stream with other people.

In one stream, Hambly says he has "anxiety diarrhea" and stepped away from the live stream leaving his guests awkwardly having to pick up the show. He comes back and discusses trying to poop before the show and his frequent usage of Imodium. In a separate stream, Hambly described when he was fishing at a state park and had to defecate in a trashcan.

The first large controversy came in August of 2020 when Hambly, in a now deleted live stream, played a video game called *Fall Guys: Ultimate Knockout.* (Virusanity, 2020) In the video, Hambly states, "My wife went out for pizza without me. And I'm angry about it." He appears to be inebriated. He struggles to stay upright, slurs his words, has a shifting mood, and repeats himself constantly. Hambly talked about peeing in his basement because he doesn't have a toilet in his basement. He then proceeds, off camera, to pee on the floor drain of the basement. When he comes back on stream, he repeats, "I just peed in my basement." The "I just peed in my basement" line became a small internet meme. It was most notably referenced by H3H3 and they frequently used it for comedic effect on the podcast's soundboard. Hambly did a good job of laughing off the affair, and it was quickly forgotten.

Hambly began livestreaming with Sydney Watson in 2022. Various clips began to circulate of Hambly acting inappropriately on stream. (Kino Casino Clips, 2025)

In one stream, he admits drinking alcohol during the stream. Watson's face appears to be annoyed. Generally, drinking alcohol while on stream is seen as casual at best and unprofessional at worst.

He went on to discuss that he receives "d**k pics" but laments the quality of the penises that he receives, noting they are flaccid and not impressive. Watson responds with, "you don't have to look at penises," and is visibly cringing at the topic of discussion. Hambly describes peeing in a trough in a public restroom and looking at other men's penises.

Hambly also discussed his bowel movements, including a section of the show where he discusses his need for Imodium. Watson asks, "What's Imodium?" Hambly then goes on to describe his reliance on Imodium. Many times, before leaving the house, he contemplates whether or not to take Imodium as he fears having accidents while out in public. Watson's mouth is agape and appears shocked and concerned at the direction of the conversation. He states he would rather deal with the constipation of Imodium than dealing with diarrhea.

"This is not information I needed," she says, and later continues to say, "This just confirms to me that men are revolting."

Later, Hambly starts reading the super chats. One of the chats says, "Just wears Depends [adult diapers]. You'll be fine." Hambly says, "that is something he's considered." Watson had a visible side eye. Hambly says dealing with gut pain is better than wearing a dirty diaper. Watson, upon hearing those words from her cohost, eyes widened and visibly cringed. (Kino Casino Clips, 2025)

Hambly started his new live stream, *QuarteringLive*, with Melonic Mac, Hannah-Claire Brimelow, and Luke Redowski in July 2025. The show is supposed to be about current events, news, and politics. Though sometimes he also uses the livestream to discuss his bowel movements and other inappropriate comments.

In a livestream with Melanie Mac, Hambly states, "everybody sh*ts their pants." And describes his BM as "soft serve after Taco Bell". He also discusses having to pre-take Imodium. He goes on to tell a story about his difficulties with using the restroom on an airplane. He would rather have "constipation over potential disaster", drawing a nervous laugh from his cohost. Hambly later reads a humorous super chat, which was a troll donation, "Chat says I'm sick of this motherf**king poop on this motherf**king plane." A humorous reference to the Samuel L Jackson film *Snakes on a Plane*. (Kino Casino Clips, 2025)

In a livestream with Count Dankula as a guest, a Scottish creator, comedian, and free speech activist, Hambly made comments ridiculing someone for being divorced. Two members of the panel, Dankula and Melanie, are divorced. His comments were met with nervous laughter, possibly seen as tone deaf. (QuarteringLive, 2025)

Later in the livestream, Dankula discusses his special needs daughter and going through speech therapy. While she has difficulty verbally communicating, she can understand what people are talking about. Hambly says, "Your daughter was asking about what double penetration was." At that moment, everyone's face becomes visibly distressed. Mac and Claire appear visibly cringing, and Dankula looks angry or bemused, then nervously laughs it off. Hambly continues by saying when Dankula's daughter was born Hambly joked, "haha one day she's [daughter] is going to be dating and having sex." He continues by saying, "still to this day he [Dankula] calls me a pedophile over that joke." Later in that video, with Dankula still on stream, he goes on a 7-minute diatribe about his channel's lack of views and how YouTube is demoting his videos.

The Trail of Smears

In that same video with Dankula, Dankula asked "how many times will you talk about pooping your pants?" People found the video he was referencing. Hambly told the story when he was doing a podcast called *The Incredible Salt Mine* around 2018, with Bearing and Count Dakula. In the story Hambly describes, in graphic detail, getting diarrhea at Walmart. (Kino Casino Clips, 2025)

DEFCRAP 5

At Walmart, Hambly describes being 32-34 years old, which would have been three years before the date of the podcast. He had just eaten at Qdoba, a Mexican fast casual dining chain. There was lots of cheese in the food he ate, and he has a little problem with cheese. He states he could feel that he was going to have a "watery sh*t" at some point.

DEFCRAP 4

He and his wife went to Walmart and near the front of the store, he could feel the urge starting to hit him. There are restrooms at the front and rear of the store. Hambly states his mind immediately goes into slow motion and starts doing the calculations on how long it will take to reach the restroom. He states, "there is a real possibility I might sh*t myself." Hambly decided to use the restroom at the back of the store so nobody would see him poop his pants, rather than take the shortest route to the front bathroom.

DEFCRAP 3

Hambly began trekking his way to the back of the store. He saw the restroom. At the moment, when he got sight of the restroom, the point of no return struck. "It's happening now. If I have to sh*t in the store, where is the best place to sh*t in a Walmart?" Hambly asks. Hambly cut into the shoe aisle, because nobody buys shoes at Walmart. Then, he felt it running down his leg.

DEFCRAP 2

Rather than kneel and accept his fate, he's decided to go for it, and make one last push to reach the restroom. Hambly was at the rear wall of the Walmart and continued traveling towards the restroom, next to the television section. From the shoe section to the TV section, Hambly began leaving a trail of fecal matter as it ran down his pants, through his socks, and onto the floor of the Walmart - *The Trail of Smears*. Hambly began running with clenched butt cheeks trying to stop the coming avalanche of diarrhea.

DEFCRAP 1

Hambly did eventually make it to the restroom. At this point, all hell breaks loose. Hambly burst open the bathroom door and quickly begins ripping his pants off.

"My underwear, it's over," he stated. The liquid diarrhea had totally soaked his underwear. "Those aren't coming home with me," he continued. He tried to save his pants. Diarrhea was still coming down his leg.

There was another man in the restroom at the urinal peeing. (Imagine, you are minding your business and taking an innocent urination while doing some grocery shopping).

Jeremy Hambly, six foot five inches and 350 pounds, bursts in and begins removing his soiled pants. The man whipped his head around at the sudden noise. "Dude, I'm sh*tting myself. I'm sorry," Hambly explained to the innocent man at the urinal. Very quickly there was diarrhea all over the floor.

Hambly finally made it to the stall. His pants remained in the middle of the Walmart bathroom, in front of the sink.

Hambly states another man came into the bathroom. He refers to him as a "cotton top". (I had to look that up. It's slang for an older African American man with a head of white hair.) Hambly describes the man as a "hero". This man began barricading the door, to make sure others did not come upon this horrific scene.

He then proceeds to "take a bath in a Walmart sink" and started to clean up the crime scene. "I had sh*t all over me," he stated.

Chased out of the Algorithm

Hamby's self-confessed stories about pooping his pants began to be widely circulated online through various clip channels, including Kino Casino Clips throughout 2025. Because they were using his name "Jeremy Hambly" and "TheQuartering" in the titles of their videos, their videos began to push Hambly's videos out of the algorithm. (Kino Casino Clips, 2025)

Hambly responded by frequently uploading to a different channel he has called: Jeremy Hambly. This channel has videos identical in style to his TheQuartering channel videos and he was successful in retaking the algorithm. As of September 2025, searching "TheQuartering" and "Jeremy Hambly" into YouTube takes you to his content, not detractor content.

It's unknown if this will continue as his views dwindle, and the troll and detractor channels grow in popularity.

The Way Down

Hambly uploaded a video called: "I'm Destroying My Channel…" on June 20, 2025. (TheQuartering, 2025) Hambly states he has anxiety over his declining channel. Videos which used to get 50,000 to 70,000 views get 10,000 to 20,000 views. Hambly expresses frustration and does not understand why his videos are not getting views.

He asked the audience what the problem was. Hambly admits the biggest complaint he received was too many ads. Ads for sponsors, the coffee, his livestream, his cookbook, etc. He also admits to deleting videos that didn't get enough views. For context, deleting videos hurts you in the algorithm. He references his low click through rate.

Let's just pause here. Hambly's corporate job was working on CRO, *click rate optimization*, so this is something he is an expert on. He briefly explains click-through rate, "the number of times people click versus the number of times the video is shown to them, the higher the click-through rate, the more YouTube will show it to people. That's why clickbait is a thing."

He also admits his content is bad and videos are boring. The article reading style of content is going out of fashion. He then states he hired a researcher full-time. He also says he had 10 employees and cut that down to three.

He promises to do better: decrease ads, increase quality, reinvigorate the channel, and spend less time on Twitter. He would be at Stage 4: Promising Change - in the stages of the lolcow. There is still a chance to turn things around and prevent himself from progressing to a further stage of *lolcowdom*.

The Hambly Paradox

Hambly's content is based around a main thesis: 1) politics are constantly intruding into our everyday lives 2) that it is a negative force. These politics ruined *Magic: The Gathering* for him, and politics and political activism will eventually ruin other nerd fandom or popular culture that you enjoy. He therefore creates a channel dedicated to cataloguing and criticizing what he sees as political intrusion. He gains immense attention and audience based on this "grift".

Are his apolitical products "grifts"? Yes. They are not meant to stand on their own and compete with other products in the marketplace. They are there for *his audience*. Let's take the coffee business for example. Hambly says he wants it to be in stores one day. Let's just assume Coffee Brand Coffee is a high-quality product worth the high cost. How does CBC compete against all the other coffee already on the market – outside of it being apolitical? Does it have a special and unique blend? It's most likely drop shipped coffee. Does it have a good story and heritage? No, it's a brand-new company. Is it local or have a good atmosphere? No, there is no physical location. (The company obscures details about itself.)

If CBC is a real product, and not a grift for Hambly's audience, why isn't it sold or marketed outside of Hambly's audience? Is it at the local farmers' market? Does it enter coffee tasting competitions? Is it featured at coffee trade shows? I could not find any marketing, promotion, or vendor selling CBC outside of Hambly's content.

Value proposition is a marketing term which describes the unique benefits of a product or service. Hambly, with his marketing background, should understand this. The problem of everything he creates is there is no unique benefit other than being a "non-political version" of whatever it is. Let's take the video game review site, for example. Do you know how many thousands of websites and people on the internet review and talk about video games? It's almost an inexhaustible amount. How are you going to stand out by *only* being apolitical? What about production design? Get your reviews published faster? More entertaining? There has to be something *unique* to help you stand out from the *millions* of other channels covering video games.

Most video game reviews are apolitical, or people navigate the politicization of it just fine. People either seek out reviewers who align with themselves politically, or they just tune out the political messaging and retain the video game review portion only. But if people can navigate the world of politicization just fine, then they don't need Hambly.

Something can't be apolitical if it's owned and marketed by Hambly. He is a conservative political figure whether he likes it or not. There is nothing wrong with being conservative, just be transparent about it. Hambly has a certain political lean and is a political commentator. Because he is selling these products, they also, by extension, become political products. If Sean Hannity, of Fox News, started a coffee company and called it "Simply Coffee" and then only promoted it on *his* tv and radio show to *his* audience, wouldn't that by definition be a political grift product?

The other reason why Hambly loses money is that he sees the products he sells for a general audience. In reality, he is selling a niche product to a niche audience. It's like Trump watches. Trump sells wrist watches with his signature on it. Nobody buys a Trump watch because it tells time, they buy it because they like Trump. This is the same with online content creators. People will forgo a value proposition if it *supports* the creator because they *like* the creator. The only people who are going to buy "TheQuartering Coffee" are people who watch TheQuartering.

So, why doesn't he just cop to being conservative instead of claiming to be apolitical? In my opinion, that's his value proposition. All other conservatives are already complaining about Starbucks, Marvel, Disney, Bud Light, or whatever. The only way he was able to set himself apart was trying to be apolitical and attracting an audience of people that were sick of politicization. This sets up Hambly's paradox:

1. As a political grifter, the only products he can sell that make money are *political* products
2. The only products he sells are marketed as *apolitical*

The more he goes after SJWs, "woke", or whatever - he becomes more and more a political grifter, but then tries to sell (grift) apolitical products. These apolitical products lose money. Or put a different way: The more you grift, the less you grift. He grifted too close to the sun.

A Fork in the Road

Let's revisit the stages of the lolcow:

1. Initial success and high standing
2. Stale content
3. Controversy that alienations fans and co-creators
4. Refusal or inability to change and the eventual failure to deliver on promises
5. Responding to trolls (this is where lolcow status begins)
6. Ironic viewership, hate watchers, and the rise of detractors

7. Cease being known for original content (algorithm only shows detractor content)
8. Irrelevancy and subsistence living

Hambly hit the one million subscriber mark in 2020, a milestone any YouTuber would dream of. This is from a channel that had 50,000 subscribers only a couple of years prior. Currently, his content is beginning to decline in views. His constant e-begging became a controversy in and of itself, and his embarrassing stories and jabs at co-hosts turned off some of the usual fans.

Now we sit at Stage 4. Hambly seems to be aware and promises to change. We'll see if he is able to pull through.

Jeremy Hambly did not respond to a request for comment. Coffee Brand Coffee did not respond to a request for comment.

Troll names:
TheQuarterPounder
TheQuarterPlanet
TheDiapering
TheShartening
HamPlanet

Other memes:
"My Channel is Under Attack!" referring to Hambly's frequent usage of criticism as clickbait.
"Brie Larson" Hambly uses clickbait with unlikeable celebrities to drive views and engagement.
Put the anti-woke takes in the bag - a reference to "put the fries in the bag". Internet slang for "shut up and do your job". Which, for Hambly, is complaining about left politics.

You can use this QR Code to go to TheQuartering's main YouTube channel:

Chapter 12: Why do Lolcows Continue?

Lolcows face many difficulties. Many complain about the constant scrutiny they are under. They have few friends or colleagues, and struggle with social isolation. These hardships may not be very impressive compared to regular people's struggles, but they are real to the lolcow. There are also real-life trolling incidents like identity theft, swatting, and harassment. Facing the difficulties they do, "why do lolcows continue to be public figures?" At any time, they can "log off" the internet and return to private life. There are financial and personal explanations.

The Lolcow Gap

YouTubers have similar problems to other public figures when they try to leave public life. If they don't have the financial resources to retire, which lolcows generally do not, they have to keep working.

YouTube's low barrier of entry provides opportunities for people wanting to get started, but the skills and knowledge required for it don't translate into other fields. Many people mistake high income with high skill level, and high skill level with economically transferable skills.

Where do you go from online content creation? What jobs are available for someone with "YouTuber" on their resume as experience? There are three possibilities: doing what they were doing before content creation, staying in the entertainment space but going to a different medium, or starting your career over.

Going back to what you were doing before being a creator would not be an option for most lolcows, because there is no "career" to go back to. Before their public career online, they were working a menial job (see Trait 3 - Self Employed, Prior Menial Job). Even Nick Rekieta, the lawyer, compared to other lawyers, had a mediocre career. Generally, YouTubers had mediocre economic prospects, gravitated towards online content creation, and focused on YouTube, instead of a traditional career.

When an entertainer is moving outside of the entertainment industry, it is based on skills they didn't gain in the entertainment industry. For example, Bill Parcels was a head coach, won two Super Bowls, and was inducted into the Pro Football Hall of Fame. Parcels retired to broadcasting three separate times. Parcels was hired as a broadcaster because of his inside knowledge of how football worked. When Parcels left broadcasting (the entertainment space) and went back to coaching (prior career) his hiring as a coach wasn't based on his experience as an entertainer but based on his prior experience as a coach. The same follows for a YouTuber.

It should be noted that those creators with successful careers prior to YouTube or during their YouTube career, are less susceptible to becoming lolcows.

The jobs that would use the skills of an online content creator are generally in the entertainment space. A YouTuber must have many hats because of their vertically integrated business: actor, writer, producer, cinematographer, editor, promotor, public relations, publisher, etc. They are the jack of all trades and the master of none. They do not have specialist knowledge or skills in any one field, making it difficult for them to be hired by any regular business. If a lolcow wanted to leave their general field, and go into a specialist field, they would be competing against other specialists. These specialists have spent years honing their craft, building their reputation, and have professional connections. It would be very difficult for them, as a YouTuber, to compete against regular entertainment professionals.

For example, let's say there was a YouTuber that made comedy/skit videos. They were successful and later became a lolcow. The lolcow wanting to leave the internet would then have to work in a different medium. Let's say TV. They would be competing against all the other comedy writers that have specialized in that field who have years of experience; they wouldn't stand a chance.

The creator, making content for his own channel, has the skills of a writer that passes his own internal quality control measures. The level of craft necessary to be a writer for your own YouTube channel is much less than the level of craft needed when competing against other staff writers working on a TV show. On your own channel, you are the writer, and you can approve what you wrote. In the real world, you are competing against someone else, and it's someone else approving it.

With no career to go back to, and no different entertainment job available, the only place to go is to start over. Starting over, whether you are a YouTuber or not, is very difficult. It would likely entail taking an entry level job, working in retail, food service, or hospitality. These are also jobs available to everyone and have low salaries.

The *Lolcow Gap* is the difference between 1) *effort* put in by the lolcow for their online content creation and the money earned from that and 2) the *effort* of working a regular job and income they could earn from that.

Most lolcows earn about the same as working a low skill job. Let's say a lolcow earns $40,000 a year. (That is a fraction of what they used to make when they were in the growth or peak stage of their career.) If they quit being a YouTuber and got an entry-level full-time job somewhere else like working in a warehouse, driving a truck, front desk agent, mail carrier, etc., let's say they could make $50,000 a year. The choice seems obvious to most people, quit being a lolcow and go get a regular job to make more money.

However, once you factor in the side benefits of being an online content creator (benefits that aren't available to people working a regular job) you start to understand why they stay in the lolcow space. These benefits include the ability to make your own schedule, work as many hours as you want, and work from home. Because you're using a computer in your own home, the environment is climate-controlled and comfortable. You don't have to wear a uniform or follow a dress code, and you don't have a boss or annoying coworkers to deal with.

For example, if you are 15 minutes late to a stream, the audience doesn't care. If you show up 15 minutes late to work, your boss will discipline you.

Let's take WingsofRedemption aka Jordie Jordan for example. There is a detractor channel which tracks his income. According to Lummox: A Hired Hoodlum, Jordan's channel donations stood (in 2025) at $3,124 in June , $4,388 in July, $4,717 in August, and $2,026 for September. Over a 4 month span, he averages around: *$3,563.75 per month.* (Lummox: A Hired Hoodlum, 2025)

Lummox also tracks his stream time: 63 hours in June, 93 hours in July, 92 hours in August, and 56 hours in September 2025. Over a 4 month span, he averages 76 hours a month. Or *19 hours a week.*

With the average monthly earnings and average monthly hours worked, we can calculate average per hour earnings: $3,563.75 / 76 hours = $46.89 per hour. (If he can make this much money in lolcow status, imagine how much money he could earn if he applied himself to the YouTube craft.) Because he only works 19 hours a week, his yearly salary is only: $42,765.00. Once you factor in income tax, self-employment tax, and having to pay for your own health insurance; (which is expensive for someone with morbid obesity) Jordie Jordan lives on a subsistence level.

Would you rather play *Call of Duty* in your pajamas for $40,000 per year or have to show up on time to the graveyard 12-hour shift at the warehouse? Would you rather stream to 200 people and get heckled with insults or be walking around for 8 hours in the blazing heat delivering mail? Would you rather work 20 hours a week making videos in the comfort of your own home or be stocking shelves, bussing tables, or cleaning messes? The choice is clear, when measured in those terms.

Being a lolcow is an easy job, which is why lolcows don't quit the internet. When you consider the comfy work they have been accustomed to, which doesn't exist offline, it's in their financial interest to stay online. Despite the pleas of financial hardship, the amount of *effort* they put in makes being a lolcow the best bang for their buck. They will stay a lolcow as long as the Lolcow Gap exits. The only way they would stop is if the gap closed and they stopped making money.

Personal Reasons

We have already covered personality flaws: entitlement, narcissism, enlarged ego, and delusions of grandeur, but in this section we will explore how these personality flaws prevent the lolcow from leaving the internet.

The internet provides them with attention. They are the center of the world on their own YouTube channel. Even a meager audience, of a couple of hundred viewers on a livestream, is mana from heaven to the attention starved lolcow. Imagine you rented out a public space, a hotel ballroom, and every single night 200 people showed up and watched you play an irrelevant 20-year-old video game, eat fast food, or bloviate about your personal problems. You would probably have an inflated ego, because no normal person would sit through something that boring. You could start to believe there was something special about you, which keeps drawing people in. And let's assume their victim narrative of trolling and intrusion is real, and constant heckling of the internet wrecks their mental health. Who would put up with that abuse while getting paid minimum wage? A narcissist desperate for attention.

A parasocial (from the Greek *para*, meaning "beside" or "beyond") relationship is a one-sided emotional bond between a media figure and audience. This phenomenon predates the internet. In 1956, sociologists Donald Horton and R. Richard Wohl described the phenomenon in their article *Mass Communication and Para-Social Interaction*. To quote from the heading of the article: "One of the striking characteristics of the new mass media - radio, television, and the movies - is that they give the illusion of face-to-face relationship with the performer. The conditions of response to the performer are analogous to those in the primary group. The most remote and illustrious men are met *as if* they were in the circle of one's peers; the same is true of a character in a story who comes to life in these media in an especially vivid and arresting way. We propose to call this seeming face-to-face relationship between spectator and performer a *para-social relationship*." (Horton & Wohl, 1956)

They go on to discuss the television and radio personas of that era stating, "The persona may be considered by his audience as a friend, counsellor, comforter, and model; but, unlike real associates, he has the peculiar virtue of being standardized according to the 'formula' for his character and performance which he and his managers have worked out and embodied in an appropriate 'production format.' Thus his character and pattern of action remain basically unchanged in a world of otherwise disturbing change. The persona is ordinarily predictable, and gives his adherents no unpleasant surprises. In their association with him there are no problems of understanding or empathy too great to be solved. Typically, there are no challenges to a spectator's self – to his ability to take the reciprocal part in the performance that is assigned to him – that cannot be met comfortably. This reliable sameness is only approximated, and then only in the short run, by the figures of fiction. On television, Groucho is always sharp; Godfrey is always warm-hearted."

Most research into parasocial relationships is from an *audience perspective*. Few have considered it from a *creator perspective*. What if a creator could have a parasocial relationship with the audience? It wasn't possible in the television and radio era because there was no way for the creator to receive constant feedback from the audience. But in the internet era, it is not only possible, but that sort of engagement is *encouraged*.

Lolcows don't have many friends offline. Is it possible the warm glow of the internet draws them like moths to a flame? Is it possible that people who pathologically substitute real-world relationships might pursue an alternative with their audience? The audience could become a source of pathological attention, validation, and companionship for the creator. It could also serve as an outlet for a creator's pathological narcissism, sense of authority, and need for control.

Lolcows find it necessary to exercise total control over their channel. Not only do they have the final word on all content decisions, but they can also only be accountable to themselves. There is no boss, and nobody can tell them what to do. They also treat their channel like their own personal fiefdom and the audience as the serfs. And they exercise that power liberally. Like a mad king, any amount of dissent can quashed immediately. They can ban people, censor chat, delete comments they don't like, and/or stop chat and comments altogether. Some even lecture the audience about their lack of financial support.

Lolcows still revel in their past former glory. These delusions of grandeur, or belief they are a special person because *they are a content creator*, will keep them coming back to the internet. Even if they accept the lolcow label, they will transform it into some special brand of uniqueness.

For example, Boogie2988 in the documentary *The Dark, Sad Life of Boogie2988*, goes to a job interview with a staffing professional. Not only does he self-sabotage the interview but after the interview he calls the documentarian and states, "I'm not going to walk into some job, when I have 4 million subscribers on YouTube. I'm one of the original YouTubers." He didn't consider the fact you could make YouTube content *and* work a job. Despite Boogie acknowledging he is facing financial ruin, he still bitterly clings to his status of a creator.

Lolcows feel entitled to their lifestyle and career. Otherwise, they could simply get a part-time job to supplement their income while still doing YouTube. If they readjusted their expectations about working, they could easily get a full-time job which paid more.

The Show Must Go On

Main Character Syndrome is not a clinical term but an internet term. It describes when someone behaves as if they are the "main character" in life, and everyone else is just a side character in *their* story.

These are the traits of Main Character Syndrome:

1. **Self-centered worldview**: Seeing one's life as the central narrative, often ignoring others' perspectives.
2. **Exaggerated self-importance**: Believing their struggles, achievements, or opinions are more significant than anyone else's.
3. **Romanticizing ordinary life**: Acting like everyday events are part of an epic or cinematic story.
4. **Attention-seeking**: Posting, speaking, or behaving in ways that keep the spotlight on them.
5. **Over personalizing**: Assuming events or people's actions revolve around them.

When someone has their own YouTube channel, they are literally *the main character*. Remember the YouTube slogan, "Broadcast Yourself"? Can it be a syndrome if it is the reality in which a YouTuber lives? And as the main character of your own YouTube channel, the end of the YouTube channel would be the end of you. Could this feeling of "ending" keep people online?

Chapter 13: Why Do We Care About Lolcows?

In this chapter, we will get into my personal opinions on the subject. I believe lolcows are not just figures that are to be pointed and laughed at. There has to be something more than that because they capture our attention. Things come and go on the internet, but the lolcows persist, and they become targets for discussion and debate. Many people online like commenters, detractors, and fellow creators invest time trying to convey real advice to help them. That advice goes nowhere of course, but if you feel compelled to offer advice, you were invested in someone.

The Tragedy of Lolcows

A Greek tragedy is a form of dramatic storytelling originating in ancient Greece. It's one of the earliest forms of Western theater and storytelling. The Greek tragedy is a play that presents the downfall of the main character, who is generally noble or heroic, due to a mix of fate, personal flaws, and circumstances.

1. **Hero of High Status:** The protagonist is usually someone important (a king, prince, or respected leader). Example: Oedipus, King of Thebes.
2. **Hamartia (Fatal Flaw):** The hero usually has a personal flaw (like pride, anger, or stubbornness) that leads to mistakes.
3. **Hubris (Excessive Pride):** A very common flaw: overestimating one's power and defying fate or the gods.
4. **Peripeteia (Reversal of Fortune):** A turning point where the hero's situation flips from good to disastrous.

5. **Anagnorisis (Recognition)** The hero realizes the truth—often too late—about themselves, their mistakes, or their fate.
6. **Catharsis:** The audience experiences a mix of **pity and fear** watching the tragedy unfold, which Aristotle (in *Poetics*) said purges emotions and teaches moral lessons.

This evolved into Shakespearean tragedy, which focused less on the gods and the supernatural, and more on human flaws, moral choices, featured complex characters, and comic relief. He frequently used soliloquies to reveal characters' inner thoughts. The key features of the Greek/Shakespearean tragedy are very similar to the pattern of lolcows as discussed in early chapters. The behavior of the tragic hero is very similar to the behavior of the lolcow. Just like a Shakespearean character has a soliloquy about his inner conflict, lolcows overshare their personal information with the audience.

The lolcows we discussed in earlier chapters all had a positive reputation at some point, had fans, were likeable, and people rooted for them. They achieved a high degree of success on YouTube, and many made millions of dollars. Then something happened, there was a turning point. Their personality flaws, which they carried from the beginning of their careers, caught up to them.

In many ways, lolcows are the 21st century's tragic figures. Lolcows are not characters in a play; they are living, breathing people. What captivated people in ancient Greece, captivates people in our modern era.

Eternal Struggle

There is a mythological idea of an "Eternal Struggle", which shows up in history, religion, psychology, and literature. There is Good vs Evil, Order vs Chaos, Truth vs Lies, Freedom vs Tyranny, Life vs Death, Creation vs Destruction, etc. This carries on into popular culture: Batman vs the Joker, Zelda & Link vs Ganon, Jedi vs Sith, etc. These ideas of eternal struggle mirror the human condition. There are conflicts within ourselves. These wars, fought inside us every day, will never be completely resolved.

There is an aspect of eternal struggle with lolcows. They eternally struggle to keep making content, stay out of the job market, remain online, and against the trolls/detractors.

There is a strangely intertwined relationship between the trolls/detractors and the lolcow. The lolcow is the object of amusement and source of schadenfreude for the trolls/detractors. If the lolcow just logged off the internet, then what would the trolls/detractors do? They wouldn't have anybody to "milk" for laughs or direct righteous anger against, and the whole cottage industry of troll/detractor channels would dry up.

Without trolls and detractors, the lolcow wouldn't have an audience, and they would quickly fade into irrelevance. Without views for ad revenue, or other financial support, they would not be able to have online careers. They might have to get the dreaded *J-O-B*. The lolcow has no unironic fans, no real organic audience, and they rely on the trolls and detractors to keep them relevant and financially stable.

Object of Amusement

For the trolls, a-loggers, and detractors, their interest in lolcows can be as simple as laughing at them. They are uniquely funny because lolcows aren't comedians. They are *the object* of amusement. They lack the self-awareness to understand what they are doing or saying is funny.

It's funny when a lolcow tells a story about how they pooped their pants in Walmart. It's funny when they have a drunken crash out with cocaine on their nose. It's funny when they fail at playing a video game and get mad. It's funny when they read a troll donation and in a split second, they begin to realize what they just read was a troll.

Many outside observers have compared lolcows to reality TV. Gamer Face Gaming, a troll channel dedicated to DarkSydePhil stated in a conversation with me, "Ever watched those 'reality shows'? DSP is like one of those but not by choice." There is a primitive drama which plays out on reality TV, but lolcows offer something better; they are real people.

Schadenfreude

Schadenfreude is a German word meaning pleasure derived by someone from another person's misfortune. Usually, the pleasure is from watching the bad guy fail.

People online *HATE* these lolcows, and their reasons for disliking them are very easy to find. They hate the lolcow because of the lolcow's personal actions (online or offline), their lies, greed, hubris, manipulation, selfishness, etc. The comments section of their videos is full of the reasons why the lolcow is hated. According to my reading of the comments section:

- DarkSydePhil is hated because of his greed.
- WingsofRedemption is hated because of his laziness and selfishness.

- Boogie2988 is hated because of his lies and manipulation.
- Nick Rekieta is hated because of his ego and neglecting his family.
- Idubbbz is hated because of his self-loathing stupidity and moral grandstanding.
- TheQuartering is hated because of his greed and slop content.

Aldous Huxley, in the introduction of *Erewhon*, said, "The surest way to work up a crusade in favor of some good cause is to promise people they will have a chance of maltreating someone. To be able to destroy with good conscience, to be able to behave badly and call your bad behavior 'righteous indignation' — this is the height of psychological luxury, the most delicious of moral treats." (Butler, 1933, Introduction)

Lolcows are hateable, and because they are hateable the audience wants them to fail. The internet doesn't just allow you to watch; it's an interactive experience. Anyone can leave a negative comment, send a troll donation, or connect with other people who share the same past-time of trolling.

Even if you simply want to watch, there are others who want to watch with you. It becomes almost like a watch party. The comments section of detractor channels or internet forums become a small internet enclave of people who have the same interests as you.

The more the lolcow suffers, the more entertainment the audience gets. What is their "suffering"? It's not actual physical bodily harm, it's safe suffering that doesn't cross the line. They scrape by on low wages, get pelted with verbal insults, and many live a lonely, hermit-like existence as they've pushed away all their friends. They have to live in the shadow of their former selves and ponder what could have been. The lolcow lives in a hell of their own creation.

Chapter 14: Lessons in Lolcows

Like the heroes of a Greek or Shakespearean tragedy, there is a catharsis for the a-logger, detractor, viewer, and even trolls in our time spent with the lolcow. The lolcows are there for us to observe and learn from their story.

I present the following 5 lessons the audience can learn from the lolcow tragedy:

1. Don't Feed the Trolls
2. Listen to Advice
3. Openness to Change
4. Take Control of Your Life
5. Quit When It's Time

Lesson #1: Don't Feed the Trolls

It may go without saying but don't feed the trolls. This is a *fundamental internet truism*. I don't think not reacting to trolling could have stemmed the tide of their career decline, but all lolcows feed the trolls. The lesson for the rest of us is that life is too short to engage with toxic people, should exercise prudence when responding to attacks, and that engagement with toxic people is sure to bring us down with them. *We should not allow toxic people to dominate our lives.*

Lesson #2: Listen to Advice

Listening to advice is an exercise in humility and self-reflection. Listening is understanding, comprehending, and considering what is being said.

Everyone needs humility. Humility is being aware of one's limitations. It has also been defined as freedom from pride or arrogance. Going back to ancient times, Abrahamic religions, Roman stoicism, and Eastern philosophy, all see *pride* as a personal flaw. Having humility is to admit vulnerable truths to yourself: You don't know everything. You are a fallible being. Other people know more than you.

Imagine the exhaustive mental gymnastics you must perform, without humility, to convince yourself that you know everything, you didn't make any mistakes, or other people are always wrong. The consequence of believing those things, in the absence of humility, is making bad decisions, which negatively impact your life.

Having humility allows you to learn and admit mistakes. This allows you to make better decisions. Those good decisions positively impact your life. *Listening and learning will improve your life.*

Lesson # 3: Openness to Change

In my research of lolcows, I was surprised by how much of the lolcow's life is dominated by the same mistakes and issues which play out repeatedly. Lolcows become stuck in a cycle, like the movie *Groundhog Day*. They make the *same* content. The *same* complaints. They have the *same* issues. The *same* mistakes.

There are more certainties in life than death and taxes, one is change. The world is changing. Change has accelerated with technology. The evidence of an ever-changing world is no clearer than on the internet. The internet changes very quickly. Trends, fads, and movements can rise and fall in a matter of months. The internet of 2000 is not the same internet as 2010. And the internet of 2010, is not the same internet of 2020, and so forth.

The evolving internet ecosystem also applies to the online entertainment content people consume. As discussed previously, once popular styles and genres of content in a few years, or sometimes just months, can become old and stale. In order to stay relevant, you have to change with the times.

This openness to change doesn't just apply to the content but also applies to the creators themselves. Most lolcows, outside of the internet, seem unwilling to change. Their inability to change is in all aspects of their life. Their personal problems, which they overshare, remain the same for years, and sometimes decades. Now, that is fine if you are satisfied with your life and want to maintain the status quo. But, if you constantly stress your problems, and many of those problems can be seen by outside observers (so we know they are real), the only logical solution is change and reform. *Don't let fear, ego, or laziness trap you; always be open to change.*

Lesson #4: Take Control of Your Life

You should apply yourself to whatever you are doing in life. Most people learn this at an early age. I can still hear my mother saying, "Always do your best." Or maybe your little league coach told you, "I want you to give 110% effort." This is something that we should learn from lolcows: *We can't control many things in life. But one thing we can control is the amount of effort that we put into something.*

When lolcows refer to their problems, they never take ownership of their situation. The declining viewers or trolling they suffer are the results of outside forces, and not because they put in less effort, fed the trolls, made bad financial decisions, or should find other income sources. If they suffer financial hardship, the audience has to bail them out. Their bad mood or insecurities, which they overshare, are the audience's responsibility to soothe.

Even if your problems are the results of outside forces, there is no choice but to take ownership of the situation and deal with it. There are real life forces like crime, car accidents, health issues, etc. anyone can fall victim to. For example, if you have your car stolen, you can't wait for the robber to return it. You must take ownership of the situation and file the police report, call the insurance company, go buy a new car, etc. You can blame someone else, the robber, but that still doesn't mean you just sit and wait. That is what a lolcow would do: cross their arms and say, "It's not my fault my car was stolen. Why should I have to deal with this when it wasn't my fault."

There are many defense mechanisms lolcows use to avoid taking ownership of their situation. The most prominent is to blame the outside forces, usually their target is the trolls. To be fair, there are many malicious trolls who engage in unethical and downright illegal activity. You cannot control that trolling, but what you *can* control yourself. You can control how you react to trolling, the information you put out on the internet, and limit the ammunition the trolls use. *What you can control, take control of.*

Lesson # 5: Quit When It is Time

So much pop culture advice is centered around the idea of "not giving up" because most success was gained using discipline, hard work, and overcoming the odds. However, there is a time and place for giving up. Knowing when to carry on and persevere is just as important as knowing when to give up or "let it go". There are some things in life that are futile. *Futility* is part of the natural world.

I'm reminded of the movie *Wargames* (1983). One of the central themes is the futility of nuclear war. In the movie, nuclear war is introduced as a "no-win scenario", but the AI programmed to go through a series of war games to simulate World War III, does not see it that way. Dr. Falken, the genius programmer of the AI, asks one of the main characters, "Did you ever play tic-tac-toe?"

"Yeah, of course," they respond.

"But you don't anymore?"

"No."

"Why?"

"Because it's a boring game. It's always a tie"

"Exactly. There is no way to win. The game itself is pointless."

The computer has to be taught the idea of futility. Near the end of the movie, (spoiler alert) it learns the idea of futility. I wish there was someone that could teach these lolcow's the idea of futility.

Lolcows do not understand the concept of futility. Confronting the trolls is futile. Trying to explain controversy after controversy and convince the whole internet is futile. Doing the same thing day after day and expecting different results is futile. Doing the same content that was successful 10 years ago on YouTube, and expecting it to be just as successful now, is futile. Once something become futile, the only winning move is not to play.

Described in a different way, *all things must come to an end*. Quitting while you're ahead is usually the wise move, rather than dragging things out. There is also a physical breaking point. This is more clearly seen in sports, as age and the physical toll of competition degrades once-great athletes into regular people. Peyton Manning, one of the greatest quarterbacks who ever played, looked like he could barely throw a football in the last year of his career. Michael Jordan, the greatest basketball player, looked diminished by the time he was playing with the Washington Wizards. Anderson Silva, one of the best MMA fighters and long reigning UFC champions, lost 7 of his last 8 fights at the end of his career. Players who stick around past their prime tarnish their reputation and legacy. Athletes who retire before their decline and in their prime, like Rocky Marciano, Calvin Johnson, or Barry Sanders, have an almost mystical quality.

Confronted with the cold reality of physical competition, most athletes can feel the physical toll of their sport on them. They aren't as fast. They aren't as strong. They can't go the distance the way they used to. At some level, YouTubers understand those same facts. The channel isn't getting the same views. The subscribers have stopped going up or even are going down. Their YouTube career isn't as "lucrative" as it used to be. They aren't as popular as they used to be.

Many lolcows used to make the front page of YouTube, but now they barely make the 1st page of the search results. The grind of content creation, the constant need to upload and live stream, stay engaged, come up with new ideas, etc. weighs on someone.

I don't know the lifespan of an online content creator. It's like the career span of an actor, writer, or other creative endeavors. There are actors with 60-year careers, like Michael Caine, and actors with 6-year careers, like Shirley Temple, but there is a lifespan. Everyone's career has a lifespan. Father Time is undefeated. *But once you know your time is up, bow out gracefully and leave on a high note.*

Lessons from DarkSydePhil

What strikes me about DarkSydePhil is the sheer luck that he had. He was at the right place, at the right time. He was making Let's Plays when there was very little competition and right before they became monetized, and then the genre exploded in popularity. This rising tide lifted his boat along with many others. Despite all these advantages, he wasn't able to capitalize on them, and his career has suffered ever since. DSP is a prime example of massive career mismanagement, both with his finances and how he operates his channel. At every step of his career, Burnell has taken steps contrary to common sense. The only thing keeping him going is his stubbornness. Burnell has a finance degree, which makes it even more puzzling how he went bankrupt. He doesn't lack knowledge or financial education; it's something else.

In my opinion, our hero's fatal flaw is wastefulness. The limited resources, career opportunities, and time on planet Earth are all wasted. He has over a million dollars in lifetime earnings on YouTube - the fruit of his labor. He was making 6 figures a year and still went bankrupt. He could be sitting on a nest egg, but he wastes money on mobile game addiction. His combative, hypersensitive, and entitled personality makes it impossible for other creators to collaborate with him. His career has been wasted. His battles with the detractors waste his time. This wasteful attitude manifests itself in the complete ingratitude he has for his fans, the financial support he receives, and other people's time that he wastes.

No money can satisfy him. No games can satisfy him. No amount of alcohol can satisfy him. The world is not enough for DSP. He could be given the world on a silver platter, and he would send it back to the kitchen for being lukewarm.

Lesson: Appreciate what you have.

Lessons from WingsofRedemption

Wings is one of the least likely people to be a public figure. He has described himself as a hermit and a private person. He could only be successful on YouTube in the very narrow period of time in which he joined. It was an accident that he became famous on the internet at all.

Wings' lack of conception around being a public figure has been a consistent failure in his online career. And that goes back to his early days when he was on *PKA*. His inability to moderate his actions based around his lack of understanding about being a public figure resulted in many of his problems. Failure to maintain a persona made him fall back on "production" i.e., his content. His content went out of style in 2015. He could have built his brand around being a "hillbilly" character, like Jeff Foxworthy or Larry the Cable Guy, but in the gaming genre. The only thing interesting about him is *him*.

<u>In my opinion, our hero's fatal flaw is laziness.</u> He always takes the easy way out, the pathway of least resistance. This pattern can be seen in his personal life and YouTube content. Being a YouTuber was easier than working a regular job, so that's what he gravitated toward. Streaming was easier than doing edited content, so that's what he did. Eating out is easier than losing weight, and which is why he does it. Not attending his grandma's funeral is easier than going, so that's what he did. Not fulfilling professional obligations is easier than completing the survival trip with Woody and Kyle, even though you don't want to.

When you always take the easy way out in life, it can't be a surprise that nothing gets done, nothing has changed, and there is nothing built.

Lesson: Put effort into life, otherwise nothing will happen.

Lessons from Boogie2988

Boogie2988 might be the most unsuccessful manipulator and liar on the internet. He reminds me of the children's stories you read growing up, showcasing how lying can spiral out of control. The liar is always revealed at the end of those stories. Just like our childhood fables about telling the truth, and how the truth always comes out eventually, the truth about Boogie2988 came out. The internet doesn't forget, unlike people's memories. If you lie a lot, nobody will believe you anymore. He ran out of places he could go, got caught too many times, and now he can't fool anybody anymore.

<u>In my opinion, our hero's fatal flaw is that his persona is built on lies.</u> He uses people's sympathy and good will to extract money and manipulate others.

He is also a cautionary tale when it comes to building your brand. To have staying power, you have to be more than a victim. Boogie built his brand on being a victim, gaining popularity by sharing vulnerabilities with the audience. The audience will root for you, but you have to actually follow through once you have them emotionally invested in you.

Lesson: Don't build yourself on lies. Don't profit from telling lies.

Lessons from Nick Rekieta

Rekieta is an interesting case study because he is by far the most professionally credentialed lolcow I cover in this book. Despite being a mediocre attorney while practicing, his creativity, grit, and charismatic presentation of the law made legal topics interesting and accessible to a general audience. His innovative style and early work deserves recognition.

The first thing that comes to mind with Rekieta is the lost potential of his career. Law *commentary* is much easier than *practicing* law; it's less work with fewer risks. Impressing a general audience with legal knowledge is easier than impressing a judge, someone who went to law school, has decades of experience in practice, and knowledge of jurisprudence. But if you can find an audience that will listen to you, you have your career made.

It's clear that Rekieta can't admit to himself his own limitations. What are his limitations? He has very limited legal knowledge and experience when compared to other attorneys. This was seen in his earliest videos discussing defamation, an area of law he did not have firsthand knowledge in. And in his involvement in the Vic Mignogna case, where he recommended an attorney for a defamation case who doesn't regularly practice defamation law. What was he thinking?

If Rekieta was simply a quack attorney who peddled bizarre legal theories, it would not make him unique on the internet. It would also not explain the implosion of his personal life. There is something deeper going on here.

<u>In my opinion, our hero's fatal flaw is he thinks he's a lot smarter than he is</u>. He thinks can explain anything and probably can justify anything to himself. Because he thinks he's very smart, if he can convince himself, he should be able to convince everyone around him.

With his word smithing abilities, he thinks that he can explain away, justify, or excuse any of his bad behavior. This, combined with his massive ego, is why anyone who does not buy into his legal theories or explanations is met with personal attacks. This is what happened to his fans, who expressed concern about his deteriorating state; he threw insults at them. Fellow Law Tubers reviewing his case, were not rebutted with case law and legal arguments, but by personal insults. It's very sad to have someone with such talent and potential, but limited experience, destroy their whole career over their insecurities.

Lesson: Don't let your ego get out of control. Remember your limitations. And accept your limitations.

Lessons from Idubbbz

Idubbbz feels like the most unnecessary paths of any of the lolcows we covered. And I'm working under the theory he is of sound mind and that he doesn't have CTE from boxing.

He looks really confused. I don't think he had a plan for himself after he stopped doing *Content Cop*. This lack of direction led him down a meandering path which didn't go anywhere. I haven't been able to determine to degree to which his wife influenced his path. Her own struggles with identity and direction mirror her husband. It's possible they both don't really know what to do or where to go.

<u>In my opinion, our hero's fatal flaw is he has no strong convictions or back bone.</u> This manifests by how Idubbbz wants to have things both ways. Idubbbz wants to be a righteous person, but he doesn't want to take any risk in taking those stands or supporting those causes. He wants to be empathetic, but no empathy is available for his enemies that he viciously attacks. He describes himself as "stoic", but also wants to share his feelings, insecurities, and be vulnerable

with the audience, and not be made fun of. He wants to have righteous anger and call out bad people, but can't handle any criticism thrown his way. While rushing off to make new friends and allies, he alienates and discards the people loyal to him. When attacked he wants others to come to his defense, but he wouldn't defend H3H3 when their family was terrorized by a false CPS report.

His lack of strong moral compass or understanding of ethics was the same person as the Content Cop, who regularly critiqued others' bad behavior – it's almost paradoxical. Idubbbz is like some actual policemen, who don't have a strong moral sense of right or wrong, they are just there to exercise their power. This was Idubbbz's "It's either all okay or none of its okay" philosophy. Once he abandoned that philosophy, there wasn't really anything there to replace it. When he was at the height of his popularity, he could throw his weight around and people would go along with him. Now that he doesn't enjoy that same status anymore, he just seethes impotently.

Lesson: When you lecture on morals, have morals. Practice what you preach.

Lessons from TheQuartering

TheQuartering is a testament to what someone with a strong work ethic can accomplish, as someone who struggles with charisma. He had a very small internet presence and a small channel, but with consistent uploads, making algorithm-friendly content, and working collaboratively with other creators, he was able to build an almost 2 million subscriber channel. His style of content was very easy to make; he was making millions of dollars a year complaining about Disney movies.

I feel like I've gotten to know everyone I've covered in this book, including their personality and have some insight into their mind. What drives them? How did they get into trouble? Where did they go wrong along the way? He's interesting because I feel like I still don't know the man.

<u>In my opinion, our hero's fatal flaw is that the only thing that drives TheQuartering is money.</u> He is constantly chasing money, getting money, and spending money. With DarkSydePhil, who also begs relentlessly and puts out boring content, at least he probably really liked video games in the beginning. The only thing TheQuartering is passionate about is growing the business.

This transactional attitude is reflected in his content having no artistic or creative expression. They are products that come off an assembly line. They are created and spit out as quickly as possible to chase the YouTube algorithm, get quick cash, and then be forgotten about. Does he really have a journalistic passion for the news and providing information? Is he invested in politics, and affecting real change in the world? Or does he want to have fun and cover popular culture topics? Are all these things the vehicle to get money and clicks by pushing the audiences' buttons? I don't know.

His e-begging and crying financial dire straits are at odds with his flexing and need to portray himself as financially successful. He has to be both a businessman with the Rolex, and the humble Midwesterner in a flannel shirt that is requesting your support.

With all his YouTube money, is he better off now compared to before he started YouTube? Does he have financial freedom? Or is he a workaholic who spends every dollar he makes, and is forced onto a hamster wheel of perpetual work? He seems dedicated to spending money, and then he has to go out and make more money. Money can't buy happiness but it can buy the freedom to go where you want, do what you want, and spend time doing what you want to be doing. The end goal of working is not money, but the freedom money provides.

He is a cautionary tale on the endless cycle of work and consumerism. His early work with claw machines, *Magic: The Gathering*, and RC cars are much more endearing because he is clearly passionate about it. But those channels never grew into a multi-million dollar empire, like his culture war/politics grift. Now, he's stuck talking about politics and current events.

Lesson: Don't let pursuit of money be your life's pursuit.

Chapter 15: Questions I Still Have

I hoped in writing this book I would answer many questions surrounding lolcows. At the end, I realized there are additional questions I haven't been able to answer.

Do the trolls/detractors and the lolcow have a symbiotic or parasitic relationship?

It's a very strange thing. Many of the trolls and detractors would want nothing more than the lolcow to be irrelevant, for the various reasons why they dislike the lolcow. This irrelevancy would metaphorically "kill" the lolcow. However, because they keep watching and trolling, the lolcow is sustained.

The lolcow wants the trolling to stop. They endlessly engage in futile battles with the trolls and detractors. Lolcows see trolls and detractors as evil. To be fair, some trolls do engage in unethical or downright illegal acts. In the lolcow's mind, if there were no trolls and detractors, they would be free and liberated from toxicity. They only want to be left alone. The problem is they don't have any regular audience, and are only relevant because of the detractors. If there were no detractors, the game would be over.

This brings us back to the question: Do the trolls/detractors and the lolcow have a symbiotic or parasitic relationship? I've thought about this in two different ways. It could be considered symbiotic because both are getting what they want. The trolls/detractors want entertainment at the lolcow's expense. The lolcow wants relevancy, viewers, and financial support.

It could also be parasitic. The trolls/detractors and the lolcow are both wasting time and money. If the goal of the troll/detractor is to destroy the lolcow, they could just leave them alone. Spending time on the lolcow and providing them with financial support, in the way of views and troll donations, are both counterproductive to the goal. And for the lolcow, they have no viable online career. What would be in their best interest, especially in terms of mental health, would be to end their online career, resign from being a public figure, and get a regular job. At the end of the day, both parties would be better off just moving on from each other.

How much of lolcow status is related to (undiagnosed) autism?

Autism, or Autism Spectrum Disorder, is a neurodevelopmental condition which affects how a person perceives the world, communicates, and interacts with others. The spectrum refers to the wide range of issues, challenges, and levels of functionality. There is also Asperger's Syndrome, which was merged with Autism Spectrum Disorder, and is considered level 1 autism or mild autism. Level 1 autism is considered highly functional but still requires support.

What are the traits of Level 1 Autism aka Aspergers? These are just a few:

- Intense focus on specific topics or hobbies
- Literal interpretation of language (missing sarcasm or social subtext)
- Difficulty reading facial expressions or tone
- Strong preference for routine or rules
- Sensory sensitivities (to sounds, textures, or lights)

- Exceptional memory or attention to detail
- Difficulty in emotional regulation

Many of these traits can be seen in lolcows. Particularly, literal interpretation of language, difficulty reading facial expressions, intense focus of specific topics/hobbies, and difficulty in emotional regulation. You cannot diagnose someone just from watching them, but the more you examine the lolcow's difficulties in understanding social interactions, it becomes increasingly apparent there must be some sort of other issue going on. You begin to wonder if they might have some sort of mild autism disorder.

Let's take, for example, Jeremy Hambly aka TheQuartering, and his stories about bowel movements. They make his cohosts visibly uncomfortable, but he continues to do it. It's possible that he cannot pick up on those hints. A troll or detractor might say, "it's his fetish", "it's a power trip", or "he's gross". It could be more fair to say he doesn't realize what he is doing. Because he is the boss and the presenter of the show, there are no checks and balances, and he doesn't get the support that he needs (if he does have autism spectrum disorder). If Hambly worked in a regular office, as opposed to YouTube, and he was in the breakroom and shared one of his "self-defecating" stories, what would happen? It would make people feel awkward, word would get around, and somebody would pull him aside and say, "Jeremy. We all like you here, but you can't tell people poop stories in the breakroom. It's awkward." He would most likely understand and wouldn't do it again.

Steven Cambian, host of the show *Truth Seekers*, also raised this question when discussing Philip Burnell aka DarkSydePhil. Cambian conducted a two-hour interview with Burnell on February 13, 2025. (Truthseekers, 2025) It was very similar to the Side Scrollers interview. Cambian pressed Burnell on many details about the bank leaks, and his alleged *WWE Champions* addiction. Cambian is also personally familiar with autism spectrum disorder because his child has the disorder. (That Being Said, 2025) He noticed some of the signs of autism in Burnell, like his strict schedule, difficulty controlling emotion, and lack of understanding around social cues and norms. Cambian asked Burnell in his interview if he was ever evaluated for autism. Burnell responded that he was never tested as a child, and it never came up in his childhood. His answer indicated he never thought you could get diagnosed with the disorder as an adult.

People with this disorder may do actions which seem rude or socially unacceptable. Their intent is not to be rude. They simply have a lack of social understanding around their conduct. The danger of being an independent content creator is it isolates people from checks and balances. People with this disorder need that extra level of support or understanding.

This would certainly add ethical concerns when dealing with lolcows. I would also agree that being autistic is not a shield from criticism. Many people who have autism don't act in the way many lolcows act.

Is lolcow status a male phenomenon?

There are very few female lolcows. It's like female serial killers, they exist but are a very small minority. What are possible explanations for this gender imbalance? In my opinion, it is because women have higher social awareness than men.

Let's use Ian and Anisa Jomha as an example. Both their stories have become interconnected, and they both would be in lolcow status, except that Anisa doesn't really respond to trolls. She might chime in here or there, but she is nowhere as combative with the trolls as Ian. Let's revisit the "Only Fans controversy". They had two very different reactions. Ian thought it was his moral obligation to stand up to the trolls. Anisa admitted she still listened to the trolls (which is a bad idea) but chose to ignore them.

This pattern played out many times afterwards with other controversies. Many online commentators have interpreted this as Anisa puppeting Ian, Ian having to take the blame for her, or some other manipulation by Anisa. What if Anisa is simply not engaging because she knows it's futile. And while she doesn't always *not* engage (sometimes she can't help it), her instinct is to *not* engage.

Will a lolcow change?

This is *the eternal question.* In my opinion, I don't think they can change, but there is still a possibility. Just because it hasn't happened yet, doesn't mean it won't happen. The lolcows we've covered, and the countless others we couldn't cover, still have an opportunity to change.

How could a lolcow change? I would point to the general lessons we covered in the previous chapter:

1. Don't Feed the Trolls
2. Listen to Advice
3. Openness to Change
4. Take Control of Your Life
5. Quit When It's Time

The real person?

How real are the people we see online? Could it be possible, once someone adopts a detractor mindset, every action taken by a creator might be seen in a more negative way? This could be considered a fundamental attribution error, where someone overestimates the role of personality, and underestimates the role of other factors when explaining other's behaviors.

For example, let's take Jeremy Hambly, and his stories that make people uncomfortable. If we view him through the lens of a detractor, and we think of him as gross, when he tells a story that is gross, we see his personality as gross. Whereas, if we see him from a neutral position, we may not detect anything and see it as a normal humorous story.

I reached out to his co-hosts for their thoughts on Hambly, and one responded, Tarl Warwick aka Styxhexenhammer666. He runs his own political commentary channel. Warwick no longer live streams with Hambly. Despite being let go from the Hambly's stream, he still expressed a positive view on Hambly. He told me Hambly was, "polite and funny in all conversations," and expressed no problems with him.

Another example would be Boogie2988. I spoke with Mike Clum about what he's like in real life. Clum directed *The Dark, Sad Life of Boogie2988,* and spent extensive time with him. He said he didn't find him manipulative. He does have issues, like discussing suicide, but he found Boogie2988 overall friendly and they still have an amicable relationship.

With more reclusive lolcows, like DarkSydePhil and WingsofRedemption, (who are rarely seen offline) we may never know what they are like in the real world. Few people have been able to penetrate their isolated world. Is it possible when they are offline, they aren't a lolcow? Could they have some normality?

Is there redemption for the lolcow?

This question has mixed answers, and it depends on who you ask. I asked many different people, the lolcows themselves, those who know the lolcow, and the trolls/detractors. What is the definition of *redemption*? I defined redemption as the rehabilitation of their reputation, and/or being able to attract unironic viewers again. Of the lolcows we discussed in this book, no one responded to me.

I received the most responses regarding Rekieta. Andrew Esquire aka Andrew d'Adesky of the YouTube channel, Legal Mindset, collaborated with Nick Rekieta many times over the years prior to the Rekieta house raid. His channel is considered part of the Law Tube genre. He told me that, "I think Rekieta has finally been honest with himself about how bad it was and he seems dedicated to turning it around." and continued to say, "I believe there is a light at the end of the tunnel for Nick and I support him where life takes him."

I spoke with Keanu Thompson, who knew April and Aaron Imholte and Rekieta before his downfall. She stated she doesn't like Rekieta because he got April into drugs, and was stringing either April or his wife along. When I asked if there could be redemption for Rekieta she responded, "Anybody can have redemption. With him it'll be tough. If he quells his obsession with Aaron and anger with me, *maybe*." And continued to say, "Aaron may have gotten eight days in jail. But Nick has a lifetime sentence being himself. And nice sunglasses douchebag." [in reference to his latest stream in October 2025 wearing sunglasses indoors]

Elissaclips (Rekieta initially laughed at her cancer diagnosis) responded to my request to comment on Rekieta. She stated, "I think Nick has another bottom to hit. Maybe he hit a version of it but I won't be surprised if he nose dives again. I don't think he'll ever get full redemption from the audience that existed at the time but I think he's fully capable of finding reasonable success again if he were to actually move on from his personal drama on his show and figure out what his next niche will be."

Sean Martin aka Potentially Criminal is another Law Tuber. He stated, "... there isn't much else to say. It's sad to see him crash and burn like this and I hope he gets better."

Sean Ranklin, the prominent troll in the WingsofRedemption detractor community, told me his thoughts on Jordan. He advised, "I don't think he will ever redeem himself. I have seen every arc since 2009 and he continually lets his fans down, no matter whatever he is doing." He goes on to say, "The weight loss surgery arc was particularly interesting because he really seemed deadset on losing the weight, leaving the internet, and getting a job. He never lost the weight, went to school, left the internet, etc."

I spoke with Mike Clum, the director of *The Dark, Sad Life of Boogie2988*. He spent extensive time with Williams. I asked him, could Williams get unironic viewership? Clum replied, "Probably not. There are no unironic viewers. He's a persona. Could Plankton from *SpongeBob* find redemption?" He continued by stating, "he was always a persona...his persona was magnetic. He transitioned from jolly fat guy, to fallen off YouTuber, to Jerry Springer [referencing his current role on *Lolcow Live*]. I don't think he'll ever have fans of his *content*. It's still people watching this *persona*."

Agent Proper, a DarkSydePhil detractor, advised me, "Redemption is too far gone. A real coming to God moment might do it, but me and some of my fellow detractors feel like that is a long shot."

Questions on DarkSydePhil

Few can match DarkSydePhil for online career longevity. What keeps him online, when so many have retired, is his financial mismanagement. He needs money. If he could retire, he would.

He will always be online, but *will the financial support always follow?* I don't see how he could be sustained financially in the long term. Burnell is 43 years old (at time of writing). If the retirement age is 65 years old, could anyone see him doing this for 20+ more years?

What would be the spark for this lack of support? I can only speculate. I think there are two possibilities. The first is that DSP snaps. If he publicly insults his fans, I believe they would abandon him. This catastrophic rebuke would destroy the "persona", and the parasocial relationship of his viewers with Burnell. The second possibility is if Burnell had a long absence, for health issues, family reasons, or some freak accident, like falling down the stairs or car accident. His biggest appeal (if you can call it that) is his constant presence online. If he were to step away for two weeks to a month, I think his audience would move on to other streamers/creators.

Some have speculated once Burnell's parents die, and he has access to his inheritance, he will stop streaming. I don't think so. His strict adherence to routine, and need for validation and attention would keep him streaming. He might stream less, but he would keep doing it. And the inheritance, unless managed in a trust, would eventually be depleted by Burnell due to his overspending, expensive addictions, and poor financial management.

If Burnell did get his inheritance and stopped streaming, this would deplete the inheritance even faster. Burnell would return to streaming once it was fully depleted. By then, his unironic viewers and trolls/detractors would have moved on to somebody else. He would have no "streaming career" to come back to.

Questions on WingsofRedemption

The only question I have regarding WingsofRedemption is, *will there be anything in his life which would force him to change*? Wings is resilient to change and dedicated to his way of life. No matter what outside forces act on him, boxing matches, marriage, fame, financial success (early career), and trolls - don't impact his dedication to his set ways. He always comes home to the modular mansion. He will always stream first person shooters. He will always be morbidly obese. Etc.

Realistically, the only thing which could upset his life would be an act of God, like a house fire, could get him out of the "modular mansion". Some have speculated some sort of health scare would push him to change. I don't believe it would. He has accepted his fate as a morbidly obese man. He has also mentioned the fatalistic Jordan family stance on health. He didn't inherit his family tradition of smoking cigarettes or drinking alcohol, as he abstains from both, but he kept the bad diet. He went through "boot camp" with Kyle. It failed. He trained with a personal trainer in his early career. It failed. He had weight loss surgery. It failed. His wife has had a recent weight loss journey herself, despite no spousal support. Her example hasn't moved him.

Questions on Boogie2988

Was Boogie2988 always a liar or did he escalate that with time? In my opinion, it was something that escalated with time, whether consciously or subconsciously.

In his early career, there was little incentive to lie. When he was an internet nobody, there was no "fame or fortune" motive. Only later, either as a "call for help" or misguided attempt to stay in the spotlight, did his lying escalate.

He isn't very good at telling lies, and doesn't plan his lies out very well. If he were a master manipulator, he would come up with better lies. A practiced and successful liar would plan things out better by forging documents, tell lies which were not falsifiable, and/or wouldn't put themselves in a position to be challenged.

Questions on Rekieta Law

So much attention goes to Rekieta's more sensational aspects that his relationship with the law gets overlooked. *How much does Rekieta actually care about the law?* There are legal topics while very important, would not be very entertaining from a public entertainment standpoint. I understand the need to present only entertaining legal topics. Throughout Rekieta's career he rarely focused on case law, statute, precedent, jurisprudence, etc. His livestreams are more of his opinions and editorializing. His more recent streams are more about responding to trolls and internet drama. When he doesn't discuss those topics, he discusses mainly politics or popular culture topics. He now wears loud suits with tinted sunglasses indoors, as a sad attempt at a "rebellious" character.

As an officer of the court, you believe in the law, its legal processes, and the authority of the court. Even if "the system" has inequities or miscarriages of justice, believing in "the law" is there. Otherwise, *why become a lawyer at all*? This is a question I would like to ask Rekieta. It seems to me that "the law" is only his playground for creative writing, where his legal theories and legal strategy are based on imagination.

Was Rekieta's degeneracy driven by going through a midlife crisis? Were his personal issues affected by his newfound fame, money, and respectability? Or both? I would compare Rekieta's fall from grace to a plane crash. There is rarely *one cause* of a plane crash. Usually, it's a cascading series of failures which override or bypass normal checks and balances.

His job, the financial limitations of a small-town lawyer, and family, were his obligations which kept him grounded. The rigid schedule and professional obligations of running a law practice were replaced with streaming. Streaming has no schedule and no professional obligations. It also fed his ego. Money started pouring in from streaming, and with this money he hired a full-time nanny to buy independence from his children.

His inflated ego, combined with his access to easy money, work flexibility, and release from familial obligations, all set the stage for him to indulge his vices. In the beginning, this was alcohol. Alcohol was his gateway drug into cocaine, whippets, ketamine, etc. His second vice was sex. He started going to gay bars and swinger resorts - *with his wife*. He started reviewing sex toys - the Balldo. Then, he got a mistress. Which escalated into him moving the mistress into his house. He was totally out of control by this point. The nanny suddenly quit, and quickly the house fell into disrepair. Within a few months of the nanny quitting, the raid on his house took place.

Anyone could lose perspective on life, be tempted by vices, and, once under the influence of drugs and suffering from addiction, anyone's life could spiral out of control.

If Rekieta never started a YouTube channel, and continued to be a small-town lawyer, *would his personal life still have imploded?* I don't think so. The constraints of running the law firm would not have allowed him the leeway to indulge to the degree he did.

If Rekieta was this "alpha male" or "Giga Chad" who was hard partying and chasing women the whole time (before YouTube fame), he would not have pretended to be a homosexual to get close to his wife. Keeping with the lolcow tradition of oversharing, his wife told a story about how he pretended to be her gay best friend, before revealing he wasn't actually gay. If he was this cool "Giga Chad" he desperately wants to be, he would have gotten a job that allowed him access to women, frequently traveled (to be away from the home), or hired a paralegal he could make advances on.

I believe, his image of the humble small town Christian family man, was genuine. If it was a facade from the beginning, he would have been more sophisticated in hiding his vices. Men who have the wife and family facade usually conceal their indiscretions. Many of the stories of him as a "player" are told by him. And listen carefully to his stories about women making advances on him or speaking to him. All the women in these stories are sex workers at swinger resorts, strip clubs, or hospitality workers at clubs or bars. He doesn't seem to understand these women regard him as a *mark*. Rekieta wants to broadcast his exploits, a sad attempt to look cool. Most men outgrow these insecurities by high school or college age.

Questions on Idubbbz

Ian's story is strongly intertwined with Anisa's. *How would Ian and Anisa's careers turned out if they had never met?* Probably exactly where they are now - living with their parents. I didn't spend a lot of time on Anisa. She had a small profile as a public figure before meeting Ian. She had limited success as a streamer and YouTuber. Because she had limited financial prospects with her online career, I think she would have probably moved back in with her parents at some point.

As for Ian, if he was never successful on YouTube, he would probably still be working menial jobs in retail or hospitality. Because he is from San Diego, a very expensive housing market, he probably would not have had the financial means to move out and would be living with his parents.

Because they are so intertwined, many have speculated about the degree of autonomy Ian has. *Does Anisa control Ian?* I think it's safe to assume Anisa "wears the pants" in the relationship. This doesn't mean Anisa is "controlling" in some sort of abusive way.

In the interview with Michael and Kate Briggs, Ian's boxing coach, they told stories about how Ian would be told when he was hungry and needed to eat. He also had body odor and bad breath. It's possible Ian, just like a child who doesn't know how to take care of themselves, won't eat, shower, or brush his teeth without being reminded. (Or told to.) Anisa has to fill this gap by telling him what to do.

Because Ian doesn't have any direction in his career, it's possible Anisa tried to influence him into a path she thought was viable, influencer boxing. After the success of CC1, they were reportedly offered seven figures for the Creator Clash brand. If they had sold Creator Clash then and there, the decision to go into boxing would have been seen as a huge success for Ian.

Does Ian have CTE from boxing? Did CTE alter his personality? Or is his mental reasoning just incorrect? While it is possible Ian has brain damage, I think the very limited boxing career he had would be unlikely to cause CTE. I believe his emotional and intellectual maturity was somehow stunted. He lacks direction in life, doesn't use prudence, didn't plan out a career trajectory, and misunderstands basic terms like "empathy" or "stoic".

How he was stunted, I don't know. The only way to know would be to speak to people who knew him growing up or for him to be psychologically evaluated.

What we don't know is what kind of "medication" he is taking or in what doses. Many of Ian's mannerisms, gastrointestinal issues, and slowed/delayed speech could be symptoms from whatever prescription drugs he is on.

Ian may also have undiagnosed autism. People with high functioning autism spectrum disorder still require support in order to navigate through life.
Please note: You cannot diagnose someone from watching them. People cannot reliably self-diagnose. People should be evaluated and diagnosed by a doctor.

Questions on TheQuartering

TheQuartering is not yet a certified lolcow. *What is next for Hambly? Will he slip deeper into lolcowdom?* Hambly is slowly fading into internet irrelevancy as his content, which is very stale, loses viewership. Something being "bad" is subjective, but I think you can objectively state his content is stale. If you don't believe me, put on an Unsleeved Media video (at random) from 2015, a

TheQuartering video (at random) from 2019, and a TheQuartering video which came out this week. *It's the same thing:* Hambly sitting or standing in front of a crappy set talking or rambling to the camera - no editing, no graphics, no script, etc.

We will know Hambly is in real financial trouble once Coffee Brand Coffee closes. Unlike other projects, like Exclusively Games or Midwestly, he sunk lots of his own money into CBC. The coffee shop or CBC on grocery store shelves has not yet materialized. TheQuartering channel will begin to go into "zombie" channel status. As the financial stress increases, and his workload to make up those financial losses also increase, his mental health will decline which makes him more susceptible to trolling. Currently, Hambly does occasionally "crash out" or respond to trolls. For him to continue into lolcow status, there needs to be an increase in trolling and him responding to those trolls.

Chapter 16: Conclusions

The biggest conclusion I have after writing this book is we can all use some time away from the internet. There's a lot of people, and I'm including myself in this, that spend way too much time online. We all need to get out and *touch grass.*

When it comes to the detractors and trolls, I'm reminded of my conversation with director Mike Clum. When we ended our conversation on lolcows he stated, "Honestly, none of it matters. These are just random people [the lolcows]. Just manage your emotional energy. I almost felt more bad for anti-DSP people then DSP. You [detractors] are really struggling. You don't have a desire to *doxx* Plankton [the *SpongeBob* character]. This is all a show for entertainment purposes only. Don't allow it to distract too much energy from you."

I would extend that same sentiment. There's no point in asking or telling people to stop. I would only ask them to consider spending time offline. Don't spend your limited time on Earth trapped on the internet trying to take somebody down. We've all seen the damage that can be done being *terminally online,* and it's evident in the lolcows. Don't think that you're immune to the internet's toxicity.

I don't see the lolcows as these Machiavellian villains the trolls and detractors make them out to be. The lolcows are flawed regular people who never should have been successful in the first place, and they bungled the success that fell into their lap. Frankly, it could happen to anybody. As we discussed in prior chapters, their success was based on their persona, not their content. Once they failed to maintain their persona, the audience left and went onto different creators.

DarkSydePhil and Wings of Redemption just happened to start making video game content very early on, when there wasn't any competition. When they started video game content wasn't even monetizable because of strict copyright laws. This is no longer the case on YouTube. The gaming genre is now one of the largest genres on YouTube, and there is more competition now than ever before. They quickly became obsolete.

Boogie2988 was a "jolly fat guy" making vlogs in his bedroom. He went viral with Francis videos. He was never supposed to be a public figure. People weren't supposed to look up to him as this inspirational figure. He was a regular guy with normal weaknesses, who spilled his guts in front of his camera.

Nick Rekieta was a strip mall lawyer in a rural town. He just happened to cover the biggest celebrity trial of the decade, which brought him instant fame, money, and the professional recognition he never received practicing law. He wasn't some great legal analyst who had insight nobody else had. He was just a small-town Christian family man who happened to be a lawyer. His underlying issues, like alcoholism and possibly going through a mid-life crisis, hit at the same time he got lots of money and attention to feed his ego.

Idubbbz got into beef with the largest YouTubers of the mid-2010s. Once he couldn't bully people online anymore, due to YouTube rule changes, his career was effectively over. He didn't have the creative talent of any of his contemporaries, who all went on to have successful careers after 2019. He wasn't able to transition into influencer boxing because he doesn't have the skill set to be a fight promoter.

TheQuartering got big covering culture war topics right at the height of anti-SJW blowback and populist MAGA wave. But his "read the article" style of videos went out of style in 2016. He does have videos that perform well *mechanically*, but not creatively or artistically. Now that his relevancy is fading, we'll see if he continues on the lolcow path.

I've come to accept the lolcows as regular people with flaws. DarkSydePhil is a story about entitlement. The story of WingsofRedemption's story about the need for work ethic. Boogie2988's story is about how lying destroys your life. Nick Rekieta is a lesson on the importance of accepting your own limitations. Idubbbz is an example of why having strong moral and ethical convictions are necessary. And TheQuartering is a cautionary tale about the empty pursuit of money.

They receive enough trolling, criticism, etc; they don't need me to pile on. *Don't mistake my restraint for acceptance.* They had done bad things, and they suffer the consequences of those actions, but I don't think any of these lolcows are truly cartoonish villains. Many people that I spoke with, who knew and interacted with the lolcows offline, either expressed sympathy or no ill will towards them.

It's also okay to point and laugh at the lolcows, and people will laugh. I hope that we don't *only* point and laugh at these lolcows. I think there is something that we can learn from their misfortune.

Acknowledgements

I want to thank everyone who contributed to this book. I reached out to many people, and I'm grateful to those who responded.

My friend Ryan designed the cover art. My friends helped with editing. Several other friends and family members also provided valuable feedback.

Lastly, I want to thank the lolcows themselves. They provided all of us with something to be entertained by and to learn from.

References

BBC. (2018, March 15). YouTube prankster jailed for shooting boyfriend dead. *BBC*. https://www.bbc.com/news/world-us-canada-43410816

Beard & Harris Attorneys at Law. (2025). *Ty Beard*. Beard & Harris. Retrieved September, 2025, from https://www.beardandharris.com/ty-beard-1

BestOfTheBad TV (Director). (2022). *TheQuartering's Apolitical Coffee Brand Coffee is Actually Woke? Say it Ain't So Jeremy!* [Film; Youtube Video]. https://www.youtube.com/watch?v=UQC3Cv9ziG8

Bonafide Boxing. (n.d.). *MICHAEL D. BRIGGS*. Bonafide Boxing. https://www.bonafideboxing.com/bonafide-bio

boogie2988 (Director). (2011). *Dramatic Fat Guy Splash* [Film]. https://www.youtube.com/watch?v=I-CaC_43cZI

boogie2988 (Director). (2012). *100,000 SUBSCRIBERS? ARE YOU KIDDING ME?* [Film]. https://www.youtube.com/watch?v=jLVz6OskLoM

boogie2988 (Director). (2013). *500,000 Subscriber Remix with Boogie2988 aka Francis* [Film]. https://www.youtube.com/watch?v=Ybq5CV-ldBs

boogie2988 (Director). (2013). *Thanks a Million* [Film]. https://www.youtube.com/watch?v=6Vw9lYFve2Q

boogie2988 (Director). (2016). *3 MILLION SUBSCRIBERS! WOOHOO!* [Film]. https://www.youtube.com/watch?v=OEjwCqFeaIY

boogie2988 (Director). (2017). *It's true, wife and I are getting a divorce. Here's whats next for us.* [Film]. https://www.youtube.com/watch?v=E60w-0q8Y0Y

boogie2988 (Director). (2017). *THANK YOU FOR 4 MILLION SUBSCRIBERS!!!* [Film]. https://www.youtube.com/watch?v=RFjcYCo6bxE

boogie2988 (Director). (2019). *LANCE STEWART CONFRONTS BOOGIE2988 AT VIDCON!* [Film]. https://www.youtube.com/watch?v=TosV9bkcymY

boogie2988 (Director). (2019). *Rambling: I RUINED my feet at vidcon rofl....* [Film]. https://www.youtube.com/watch?v=5MK9T7Q3RoY

boogie2988 (Director). (2021). *I Am Finally RICH - How Crypto Made Me Rich* [Film]. https://www.youtube.com/watch?v=IAjf8giyzx8

boogie2988 (Director). (2022). *I Have A Rare Form Of Cancer.* [Film]. https://www.youtube.com/watch?v=VB-ugpL2WdQ

boogie2988 (Director). (2022). *I need your help.* [Film]. https://www.youtube.com/watch?v=VrE3bLeSSik

Brighty Gamer (Director). (2019). *Boogie2988 begs and manipulate his Viewers for money to buy a $100K Tesla* [Film]. https://www.youtube.com/watch?v=SRGadd5jxWo

Butler, S. (1933). *Erewhon.* Limited Editions Club.

Clum, M. (Director). (2023). *The Dark, Sad Life of Boogie2988 | Official Documentary* [Film]. https://www.youtube.com/watch?v=_QgDx0RIWY8

Coffee Brand Coffee. (2025). *Coffee Brand Coffee.* Coffee Brand Coffee. Retrieved September, 2025, from https://coffeebrandcoffee.com/?srsltid=AfmBOoois w5kwe2RsK0Fa7nMaKho7u0S572ki0_xWZwZkrN 05LBR0jKy

Cushing, T. (2022, August 29). *Texas Appeals Court Upholds Dismissal Of Voice Actor's Bogus*

Defamation Lawsuit. techdirt. Retrieved September, 2025, from https://www.techdirt.com/tag/ty-beard/

Davinci Virtual. (2025, 11 11). *Reserve your virtual office address at North Water Street*. Davinci Virtual. https://www.davincivirtual.com/loc/us/wisconsin/milwaukee-virtual-offices/facility-3555

Davis, C. (2025). *Defamation Law: Understanding and Avoiding the Streisand Effect*. Chicago Business Litigation Lawyers. Retrieved November 11, 2025, from https://www.thebusinesslitigators.com/business-commercial-litigation/defamation-libel-slander-and-cyber-smear/defamation-law-understanding-and-avoiding-the-streisand-effect/

DeFranco, P. (Director). (2019). *UHOH! Youtube's New CRACKDOWN, iDubbbz Content Cop REMOVED, Viral Slapper Exposed, Anthony Padilla &* [Film]. https://www.youtube.com/watch?v=u4DKKDS4k20

Destiny (Director). (2024). *Boogie Admits Fake Cancer Diagnosis, Gets FIRED & Grabs Kn*fe In HEATED Confrontation* [Film]. https://www.youtube.com/watch?v=Jql318k4Tmc

Donna (Director). (2019). *IDubbbz: Goodbye Content Cop | The Importance of Context* [Film]. https://www.youtube.com/watch?v=WeFNHwuottM

DSPGaming (Director). (2025). *The FULL Kino Casino Snaking Saga ENDS! March 19, 2025* [Film]. https://www.youtube.com/watch?v=OY1S0ZY5JIM

elissa clips (Director). (2025). *Elissa Clips Made a Health Announcement (Jun 5, 2025)* [Film]. https://www.youtube.com/watch?v=VVDs7ElOtpc

Eric Hunley (Director). (2021). *Jeremy Hambly of The Quartering* [Film]. https://www.youtube.com/watch?v=ciSCnfCG5d4

Exclusively Games (Director). (2019). *An Update On Exclusively Games* [Film]. https://www.youtube.com/watch?v=nA7y6dd5T-8

Exclusively Games (Director). (2020). *The Future Of Exclusively Games* [Film]. https://www.youtube.com/watch?v=7RNlrw5rlW0&t=67s

Featherly, K. (2019, November 26). Legal News > Your source for information behind the law. *Legal News > Your source for information behind the law.* https://www.legalnews.com/Home/Articles?DataId=1481697

Foster, B. (1953, November 7). From 'B' Pictures to Top TV Stardom. *San Mateo Times.*

Graham Stephan (Director). (2021). *My Response To iDubbbzTV | The Full Story* [Film]. https://www.youtube.com/watch?v=G3rs2rizX14&t=249s

h3h3Productions (Director). (2025). *My Response To iDubbbz's Content Cop* [Film]. https://www.youtube.com/watch?v=bHlq4Nb93vQ

H3 Podcast (Director). (2019). *YouTube Removes iDubbbz Content Cop - H3 Podcast #166* [Film]. https://www.youtube.com/watch?v=UE-6zvdRapY

H3 Podcast (Director). (2023). *Israel vs Gaza - Leftovers #61* [Film]. https://www.youtube.com/watch?v=JFznOHunD_c

H3 Podcast (Director). (2025). *Ethan Reacts To Idubbbz Content Cop - H3 Show #136* [Film]. https://www.youtube.com/watch?v=WZbGjnOT9Mc&t=379s

H3 Podcast (Director). (2025). *Ian & Anisa's Boxing Coach CALLS IN LIVE, Shocking New Details - H3 Show*

#154 [Film].
https://www.youtube.com/watch?v=bvmJr2FNgFs

H3 Podcast (Director). (2025). *Snark Called Child Protective Services On Us - H3 Show #119* [Film]. https://www.youtube.com/watch?v=ZDnseOSdk_8

Hale, J. (2021, July 27). *WingsOfRedemption stripped of Twitch partnership for violating contract.* Dexerto. https://www.dexerto.com/entertainment/wingsofrede mption-stripped-of-twitch-partnership-for-violating-contract-1619477/

Hammer, C. (Director). (2023). *Caleb Hammer Exposes Boogie2988 | Financial Audit* [Film]. https://www.youtube.com/watch?v=i5hv1YNcYII

Hedonism II. (2025). *Hedonism II.* Hedonism II | All-Inclusive, Adults-Only Resort in Negril, Jamaica. Retrieved September, 2025, from https://hedonism.com/

Herren, W. (2025, September 30). Ostracized from terrestrial radio, pretend morning DJ, Aaron Imholte, gets 15 days in jail for disseminating revenge porn; tells court behind tears, 'all praise be to Jesus Christ, may God have mercy on my soul'. *NewsFox15*. https://www.kadn.com/news/national/ostracized-from-terrestrial-radio-pretend-morning-dj-aaron-imholte-gets-15-days-in-jail-for/article_e67b20ed-6e7f-44b9-ae9e-a7398b2676cd.html

Hipsters Staff. (2017, December 7). Jeremy Hambly, aka MTGHeadquarters, Suspended Indefinitely from the DCI. *Hipsters of the Coast*. https://www.hipstersofthecoast.com/2017/12/jeremy -hambly-aka-mtgheadquarters-suspended-dci-mtg/?utm_source=chatgpt.com

Horton, D., & Wohl, R. R. (1956). Mass Communication and Para-Social Interaction: Observations on

Intimacy at a Distance. *Psychiatry: Journal for the Study of Interpersonal Processes, 19*(3), 215-229. https://www.participations.org/03-01-04-horton.pdf

The Iced Coffee Hour Clips (Director). (2024). *Caleb Hammer Exposes Boogie2988 LIES* [Film]. https://www.youtube.com/watch?v=mxcUgidwMEQ

iDubbbzTV. (n.d.). *iDubbbzTV*. Youtube. https://www.youtube.com/@iDubbbzTV

iDubbbzTV (Director). (2017). *Content Cop - Tana Mongeau* [Film]. https://www.youtube.com/watch?v=Yb3UpY7jgKM

iDubbbzTV (Director). (2020). *Sex-workers - idubbbz complains* [Film]. https://www.youtube.com/watch?v=mQLzOuwDu_ 8

iDubbbzTV (Director). (2022). *How I feel about my loss... (+Announcement)* [Film]. https://www.youtube.com/watch?v=Q6-ybNjUe6A&t=5s

iDubbbzTV (Director). (2023). *Addressing the Froggy Fresh Drama* [Film]. https://www.youtube.com/watch?v=ROlvcNFYCUs &t=1049s

iDubbbzTV (Director). (2023). *The Harsh Reality of Creator Clash 2* [Film]. https://www.youtube.com/watch?v=5VZ084lzyBo& t=422s

iDubbbzTV (Director). (2023). *"I miss the old idubbbz"* [Film]. https://www.youtube.com/watch?v=iRkCfOuW_u0 &t=421s

iDubbbzTV (Director). (2025). *Coming clean...* [Film]. https://www.youtube.com/watch?v=wUcXHcOfpFk &t=2s

iDubbbzTV (Director). (2025). *Content Cop - H3* [Film].
https://www.youtube.com/watch?v=NyB85pVw-v4

iDubbbzTV (Director). (2025). *Creator Clash is back* [Film].
https://www.youtube.com/watch?v=B_leuDRGB10

Jomha, A. (Director). (2020). *Do I regret making an onlyfans?* [Film].
https://www.youtube.com/watch?v=ewaMLIVPQKg

Joon The King (Director). (2019). *From Massive To Passive - Boogie2988's Story (Steven Williams)* [Film].
https://www.youtube.com/watch?v=VRZEFxVsmDU

Joon The King (Director). (2023). *The Continual Fall Of Boogie2988 - 2023* [Film].
https://www.youtube.com/watch?v=qTjH2PKedzI

Jordan, J. (2021, October 9). *Twitter*. @WORGODICP.
https://x.com/WORGODICP/status/1446913756873863170

Kino Casino Clips (Director). (2025). *DARK SYDE PHIL GETS SNAKED! ALL BRIDGES BURNT!* [Film].
https://www.youtube.com/watch?v=RWw44KeHvSM

Kino Casino Clips (Director). (2025). *THE DENTED ZONE (A DarkSydePhil Parody Movie)* [Film].
https://www.youtube.com/watch?v=pS4qbC6T7bs

Kino Casino Clips (Director). (2025). *Jeremy Hambly AKA The Quartering FURIOUS Over Kino Casino Hijacking His Name!* [Film].
https://www.youtube.com/watch?v=f3Ni7rityOo

Kino Casino Clips (Director). (2025). *NICK REKIETA DYING FROM HUFFING GALAXY GAS! BLUE FINGERS! + COPE STREAM!* [Film].
https://www.youtube.com/watch?v=_15LfcfsDX0&t=1689s

Kino Casino Clips (Director). (2025). *THE QUARTERING POOPS HIS PANTS AT WALLMART!* [Film]. https://www.youtube.com/watch?v=Iup9Twj2d7E&t =3520s

Kino Casino Clips (Director). (2025). *The Quartering SIMPS Hard for Sydney Watson + Baldur's Gate 3 Disaster!* [Film]. https://www.youtube.com/watch?v=35wGacn5AhU &t=2125s

Kino Casino Clips (Director). (2025). *THE QUARTERING STRUGGLES! LEAVES SYDNEY WATSON TRAUMATISED!* [Film]. https://www.youtube.com/watch?v=_LU1rlddbCs&t =4278s

Kino Casino Clips (Director). (2025). *THE QUARTERING VIEWERS HAVE HAD ENOUGH OF HIS ENDLESS BEGGING! USES CO HOSTS FOR EXTRA CASH!* [Film]. https://www.youtube.com/watch?v=1AuEiQGySS8 &t=2610s

Kluster (Director). (2025). *The Full Story of Boogie2988's Arrest* [Film]. https://www.youtube.com/watch?v=L99io-zOiK0

Knudsen, F. (Director). (2019). *WingsOfRedemption | Down the Rabbit Hole* [Film]. https://www.youtube.com/watch?v=LNHbm7GBHw g

KYM. (2020, March 13). *Anisa Jomha's OnlyFans*. Know Your Meme. Retrieved September, 2025, from https://knowyourmeme.com/memes/anisa-jomhas-onlyfans#fn1

LolcowLive (Director). (2025). *Fat Camp - Day 6 - TTS 😵 Truth or Dare ❗ 😆* [Film]. https://www.youtube.com/watch?v=QyNGul6U_48

Lorenz, T. (2018, October 12). *YouTube Stars Are Being Accused of Profiting Off Fans' Depression.* The Atlantic.
https://www.theatlantic.com/technology/archive/201
8/10/youtube-stars-accused-of-profiting-off-
depression-betterhelp-shane-dawson-phillip-
defranco-elle-mills/572803/

Lummox: A Hired Hoodlum. (2025). *Lummox: A Hired Hoodlum.* Youtube. Retrieved September, 2025, from
https://www.youtube.com/@LummoxAHiredHoodlu
m/posts

National Coffee Association of USA, Inc. (2025, April 15). *More Americans Drink Coffee Each Day Than Any Other Beverage, Bottled Water Back in Second Place.* National Coffee Association. Retrieved September, 2025, from
https://www.ncausa.org/Newsroom/More-
Americans-Drink-Coffee-Each-Day-Than-Any-
Other-Beverage-Bottled-Water-Back-in-Second-
Place

Nobody Likes Onions (Director). (2025). *THIS LITTLE PIGGY: A Steel Toe Roundtable Discussion (May 23, 2025)* [Film].
https://www.youtube.com/watch?v=J6ZTYDPmUB
c&t=11628s

Osborn, A. (2016, December 1). *The Game Awards 2016 Winners Announced.* IGN. Retrieved November 11, 2025, from
https://www.ign.com/articles/2016/12/02/the-game-
awards-2016-winners-announced

PKA Clips (Director). (2024). *The Best of WingsofRedemption on PKA (Compilation)* [Film].
https://www.youtube.com/watch?v=-MpgHVDBrsw

Potentially Criminal (Director). (2025). *Steel Toe Plea Deal Show, Trump Legal Updates, Florida Boat Burglary, and more!* [Film]. https://www.youtube.com/live/r2dJ1Wj2W_E

The Publica (Director). (2023). *Welcome To ThePublica* [Film]. https://www.youtube.com/watch?v=pO4yz0VXlro

PublicRecords, M. (2024, June 18). *MNPublicRecords CHIPS file on Rekieta's 9-year-old testing positive for cocaine - All parties are assumed innocent until proven guilty in a court of law.* Kiwi Farms. https://kiwifarms.st/threads/mnpublicrecords-chips-file-on-rekietas-9-year-old-testing-positive-for-cocaine.193896/

QuarteringLive (Director). (2025). *Count Dankula Live On Migrant Crisis In Europe, Whiteness & More* [Film]. https://www.youtube.com/watch?v=m-j6QsR2EPM

Ranklin, S. (Director). (2019). *WingsofRedemption gets stream sniped and loses it - Sean Ranklin Reupload (1080p)* [Film]. https://www.youtube.com/watch?v=TLpEHfpgFFw

Rekieta, N. (2025). *Nicholas Rekieta*. LinkedIn. Retrieved September, 2025, from https://www.linkedin.com/in/nicholas-rekieta-a0969069

Rekieta Law. (n.d.). *Rekieta Law*. YouTube. Retrieved September, 2025, from https://www.youtube.com/@RekietaLaw

Rekieta Law. (2025, June 3). *@RekietaLAw*. Twitter. Retrieved November 11, 2025, from https://x.com/RekietaLaw/status/1929981521991217644

Rekieta Law. (2025, July 30). *Rekieta Law*. Facebook.
    Retrieved September, 2025, from
    https://www.facebook.com/RekietaLaw/

Rekieta Law. (2025, September). *Rekieta Law*. twitch.tv.
    Retrieved September, 2025, from
    https://www.twitch.tv/rekietalaw

Rosenblatt, K. (2022, December 19). Johnny Depp and
    Amber Heard defamation trial: Summary and
    timeline. *NBC News*.
    https://www.nbcnews.com/pop-culture/pop-culture-
    news/johnny-depp-amber-heard-defamation-trial-
    summary-timeline-rcna26136

Rumble, Inc. (2023, January 4). Rekieta Law Joins Rumble
    Exclusives Popular legal commentator joins Russell
    Brand, Glenn Greenwald and Dave Rubin by
    moving his full livestream exclusively to Rumble.
    GlobeNewswire.
    https://www.globenewswire.com/news-
    release/2023/01/04/2582960/0/en/Rekieta-Law-
    Joins-Rumble-Exclusives.html

Samuelson, A. (2012, September 14). Dana White Blames
    Injury Woes on 'Horrible (Expletive) Luck'. *SB
    Nation*.
    https://www.mmafighting.com/2012/9/14/3331766/d
    ana-white-blames-injury-woes-on-bad-
    luck?utm_source=chatgpt.com

Seethin Steven (Director). (2024). *McJuggerNuggets and
    KidBehindaCamera reveal Boogie2988's s*icide
    threats at Vidcon 2019* [Film].
    https://www.youtube.com/watch?v=C-Sk4sw8q8E

Seethin Steven (Director). (2025). *Boogie2988 laughs about
    traumatizing dozens of people at Vidcon 2019 with
    s*icide threats* [Film].
    https://www.youtube.com/watch?v=79i7S5YkJYQ

Side Scrollers (Director). (2023). *DarksydePhil Interview |
Side Scrollers Podcast | March 16th, 2023* [Film].
https://www.youtube.com/watch?v=yQw-IxvvE6c

Smith, J. (2020, January 31). *Bankruptcy Analysis and FAQ
Thread*. Kiwi Farms.
https://kiwifarms.st/threads/bankruptcy-analysis-
and-faq-thread.65795/

Social Blade. (2025). *boogie2988*. socialblade.
https://socialblade.com/youtube/channel/UC4_bwov
47DseacR1-ttTdOg

Social Blade. (2025, September). *TheQuartering*. Social
Blade. Retrieved September, 2025, from
https://socialblade.com/youtube/handle/thequarterin
g

Social Blade. (2025, September). *Wings of Redemption*.
Social Blade. Retrieved September, 2025, from
https://socialblade.com/youtube/channel/UCk-
xZQ9v9ZyNc9qCunW0jzQ

*SOI Tax Stats - Individual statistical tables by tax rate and
income percentile | Internal Revenue Service*. (2025,
March 26). IRS. Retrieved November 11, 2025,
from https://www.irs.gov/statistics/soi-tax-stats-
individual-statistical-tables-by-tax-rate-and-income-
percentile

Stallyn19 (Director). (2025). *Potentially Criminal: Aaron
Imholte v. Nick Rekieta HRO Hearing Recap -
8/29/25* [Film].
https://www.youtube.com/watch?v=k8gZmlTCoLM
&t=137s

SWC Backup (Director). (2025). *Nick Rekieta body cam
transcript (w/coda mirror)* [Film].
https://www.youtube.com/watch?v=1rw6c9q3xU0

That Being Said (Director). (2025). *That Being Said #150 -
The Darkest Night ft. @Truthseekershow*

@*BroSydePhil* [Film].
https://www.youtube.com/watch?v=U3Sw6cPrUPU

TheQuartering (Director). (2017). *Top 5 ShoeOnHead & Armoured Skeptic Moments At #Mythcon* [Film].
https://www.youtube.com/watch?v=YVhhvNrioM0

TheQuartering (Director). (2017). *Why Are There So Many SJW's In Magic The Gathering?* [Film].
https://www.youtube.com/watch?v=8tS4MVcbfGY&t=51s

TheQuartering (Director). (2018). *Boogie2988 Fired For Our Relationship* [Film].
https://www.youtube.com/watch?v=HdEna-QXkc8

TheQuartering (Director). (2018). *MILO & JEREMY DOUBLE TEAM MAGIC THE GATHERING* [Film].
https://www.youtube.com/watch?v=RYgBP8GF7j4

TheQuartering (Director). (2019). *DarksydePhil (DSP) Interview* [Film].
https://www.youtube.com/watch?v=ynWQxASVthg

TheQuartering (Director). (2020). *I Am AFRAID To Reach 1 Million Subscribers...But...* [Film].
https://www.youtube.com/watch?v=OlKv9g_5egU&t=328s

TheQuartering (Director). (2020). *One Million Subscribers! We Did It & Game Journos MELTDOWN Over It!* [Film].
https://www.youtube.com/watch?v=EsVt2DScsZ4&t=2s

TheQuartering (Director). (2022). *Brie Larson BLASTED By The Media!! Called A Friendless LOSER & Lame! Captain Marvel Star Blasted!* [Film].
https://www.youtube.com/watch?v=TwkW4o9Vlys

TheQuartering (Director). (2024). *Jimmy Kimmel Epstein DISASTER Gets WORSE! Old DISGUSTING Comments Resurface & GO VIRAL!* [Film].

https://www.youtube.com/watch?v=eQpXLs95rMg
&t=1s

TheQuartering (Director). (2024). *Today Sucks...Just Had To Lay Off An Entire Team...Please Hear Me Out Until The End* [Film]. https://www.youtube.com/watch?v=fHJ4f9ziLWA

TheQuartering (Director). (2025). *I'm Destroying My Channel...* [Film]. https://www.youtube.com/watch?v=pJeD17KedIs

TheQuartering (Director). (2025). *Woke Leftists Just SCREWED Me Over & All My Staff...* [Film]. https://www.youtube.com/watch?v=7-gbLGugdhk

Truthseekers (Director). (2025). *Interviewing the most controversial people on the internet! Darksydephil interview.* [Film]. https://www.youtube.com/watch?v=U5RG8zOXbCQ&t=1112s

UnsleevedMedia (Director). (2018). *Magic The Gathering Artists Boycott Events* [Film]. https://www.youtube.com/watch?v=HJ0GXk5Z2M0

Virusanity (Director). (2020). *Jeremy (TheQuartering) pees on his basement floor (August 17, 2020)* [Film]. https://www.youtube.com/watch?v=jzZm_2S3u5E

voidzilla (Director). (2024). *confronting boogie2988 on crypto scam* [Film]. https://www.youtube.com/watch?v=RqgvBSoiWNQ

Waifu, H. (2019, February 27). *Nicholas Robert Rekieta / Rekieta "Law" / Actually Criminal / @NickRekieta.* Kiwi Farms. Retrieved September, 2025, from https://kiwifarms.st/threads/nicholas-robert-rekieta-rekieta-law-actually-criminal-nickrekieta.53871/

Williams, S. B. (2020, January). *@Boogie2988.* Twitter. https://imgur.com/3ilJsNN